The Republic Fights Back: The Franco-German War 1870-1871 Volume 2

Uniforms, Organisation and Weapons of the Armies of the Republican Phase of the War

Ralph Weaver

Helion & Company

Helion & Company Limited
Unit 8 Amherst Business Centre
Budbrooke Road
Warwick
CV34 5WE
England
Tel. 01926 499 619
Email: info@helion.co.uk
Website: www.helion.co.uk
Twitter: @helionbooks
Visit our blog at blog.helion.co.uk

Published by Helion & Company 2023
Designed and typeset by Mach 3 Solutions Ltd ((www.mach3solutions.co.uk)
Cover designed by Paul Hewitt, Battlefield Design (www.battlefield-design.co.uk)

ISBN 978-1-915070-50-0

British Library Cataloguing-in-Publication Data.
A catalogue record for this book is available from the British Library.

For details of other military history titles published by Helion & Company Limited contact the above address or visit our website: http://www.helion.co.uk.

We always welcome receiving book proposals from prospective authors.

Contents

Preface

The Franco–German War of 1870–1871 was the last of the 'Dynastic' wars that had plagued Europe for the preceding 500 years. Two key players jostled for pre-eminence: Napoleon III, with his goal of maintaining the political dominance of France; and Bismarck, whose aim was to raise Prussia to that position by absorbing Germany within the Hohenzollern monarchy. Both were political schemers, but while Napoleon was incompetent and gullible and a vague dreamer with no fixed idea of what and how to achieve France's 'destiny', Bismarck was single-minded and resolute in his aims.

After Sedan, Bismarck had little further direct interest in pursuing the war and hoped for a speedy end. It had served his purpose of removing France from any influence on German unity (just as the War of 1866 had removed Austria from its former role as the arbiter of Germany). In any event, he had his hands full with ensuring King Wilhelm kept to the plan and with keeping Crown Prince Frederick and his liberal-minded friends away from government.

The momentous events of 1870 and 1871, the war between the French Empire and Prussia followed immediately by the war between the French Republic and Germany, later the German Empire, have been covered in many sources between then and now. But how were the contending forces organised, how did they fight and how were they armed and equipped? This book sets out to explain how the French built new armies to carry on the struggle, which in effect was made up of several almost unconnected campaigns.

The Germans were convinced that the capture of Paris would force whatever government France had to the table to discuss terms of peace. How to conquer Paris, an enormous city of two million people with vast industrial resources, was the question the German leaders argued at their headquarters at Versailles. There was no way to build siege lines and assault the city in the conventional way, there were not enough troops in the whole of Germany to accomplish that. So, to blockade the city and starve it into submission, or to bring up the really big guns and batter down its forts? In the end, a combination of both proved to be the answer, but only after all hope of outside relief was extinguished.

With Paris the centre of attention for the Germans, the French government in Tours and later Bordeaux (the Germans were too close to the former city to be comfortable) also became fixed on how to relieve the city. The main action was concentrated in the valley of the River Loire where new armies were hastily formed and flung in the direction of the capital. Another army was formed in the far north of France, not yet occupied by German forces, and names which would later be in the headlines in 1914 to 1918 – Amiens, Bapaume, and the River Somme – were fought over. In the east, Garibaldi, stirred from his new role as an Italian statesman, offered his services as a general to the new Republic. In the west the province of Brittany raised a large force of men to form yet another army to free Paris, aided by fellow countrymen in Normandy.

The Germans also found themselves having to raise more and more troops, not just to hold tight to Paris, but to fend off the new armies on the Loire, the small, but dangerous Army of the North and Garibaldi's international volunteer army, as well as to protect their supply lines and govern those departments they now occupied.

Introduction

The Battle of Sedan and the surrender of the French Army on 2 September 1870 was both an end and a beginning. News of the defeat and capture of the emperor led to a revolution in Paris with the imperial government seemingly powerless to counter the voices of the Republican agitators, who to their great surprise now found themselves the new rulers of France – or Paris at any rate. It may be remarked that what happened in Paris generally dictated (literally) what went on in the rest of the country. Lyon, France's second city at the time, generally tried to imitate the capital, but nothing on the same scale. The provinces had little influence and the populations there were more concerned with what happened locally than with events on a national scale. While Paris, having to deal with a Republican-minded mob, saw a new direction for governing France, the provincials were generally either Bonapartist, monarchist (favouring either the Bourbon or Orleanist lines) or indifferent. As an example, during the Revolution of 1792 most of France followed Paris and embraced the Republic while distant country areas such as the Vendee region took up arms against the authority of the capital. It was true that the empire had lost much of its prestige in the years before 1870, Napoleon III toyed with the idea of a 'liberal empire' and introduced some measures giving the people more freedom, but this led to less support for the government rather than increasing its popularity. The army, the mainstay of the imperial power, was also losing its faith in its leader.

As Lamartine said it was Napoleon – not the French Army – that was conquered at Waterloo, so we may declare that it was the system of the Second Empire – not the deficiencies of the French nation – that entailed the disasters of the late war, culminating at Sedan. And, in that supreme moment of peril for the country, imperialism stood aghast – without counsel, without action! It has been truly remarked that no one who witnessed the events of 4 September 1870 in Paris can possibly forget the pusillanimity of all the Bonapartists on that occasion. The *Corps Legislatif*, the Senate, their Presidents all collapsed without making a stand for the government to which they had sworn allegiance. And when it is now said that the Second Empire was overthrown by an ambush, by worthless political marauders, those who utter this taunt should be reminded that the leaders of the fallen dynasty acquiesced in their overthrow and did nothing but run away. In other words, the empire of the Bonapartes, at this vital juncture, lost its corporate political nerve.

The new 'Government of National Defence' was created on 4 September and vowed to carry on the war when good sense should have made them seek peace. It now became a matter of principle that France should exert every effort to continue the fight and that Paris, now a target for the German forces, should be saved at all costs. Thus, sound political sense was buried under Republican rhetoric, patriotic speeches and muddled military mayhem.

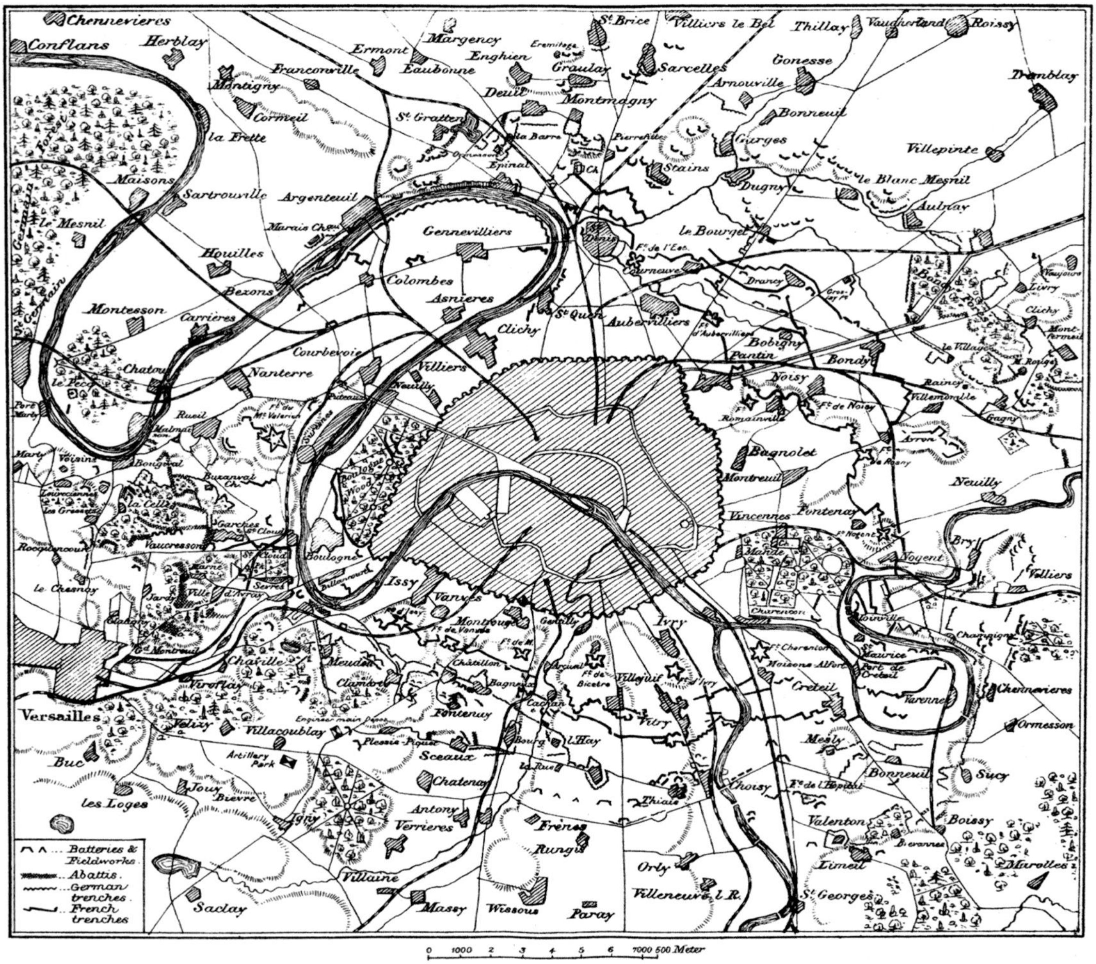

Paris and its environs.

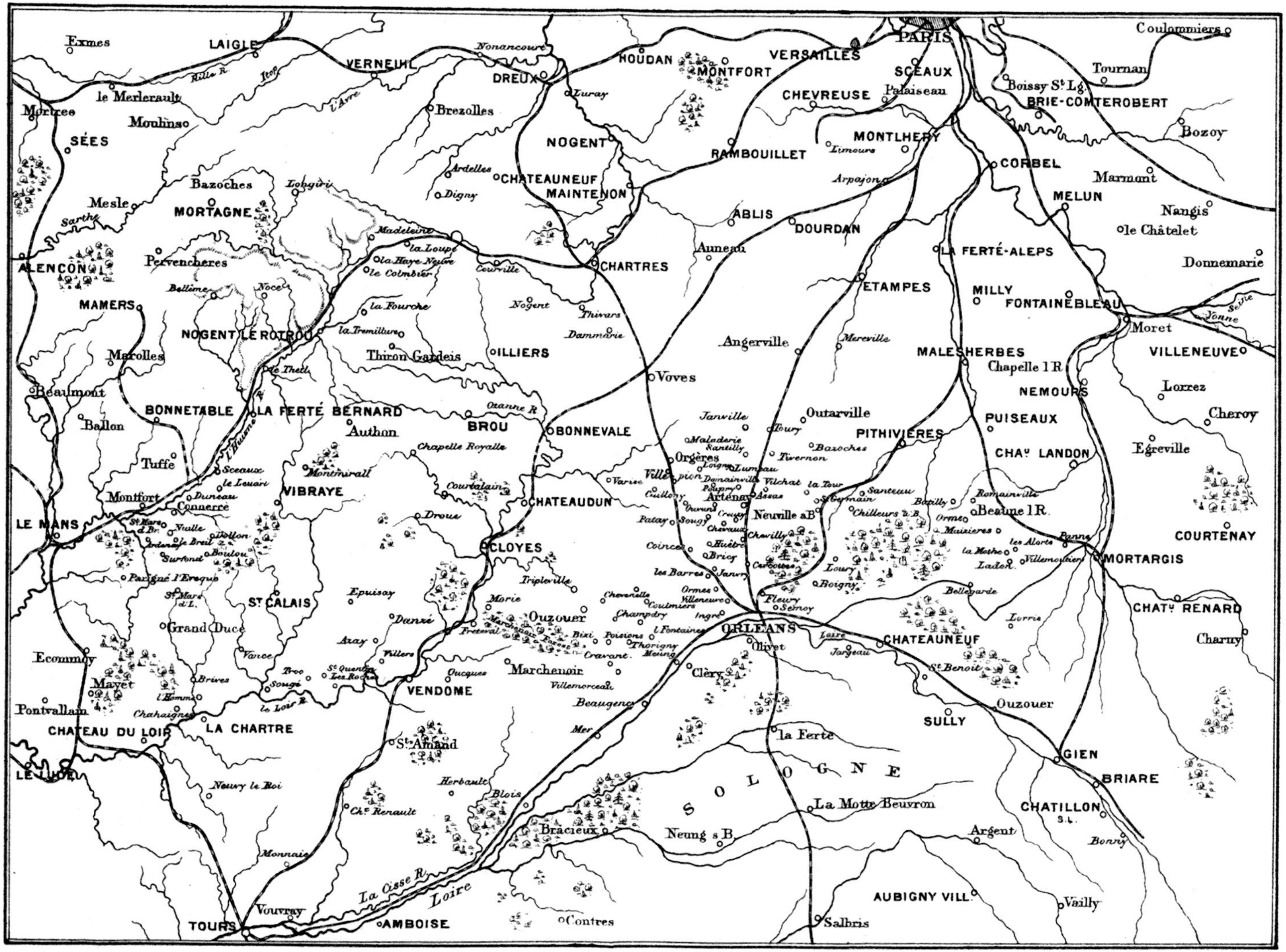

The Western theatre of war - Orleans and Le Mans.

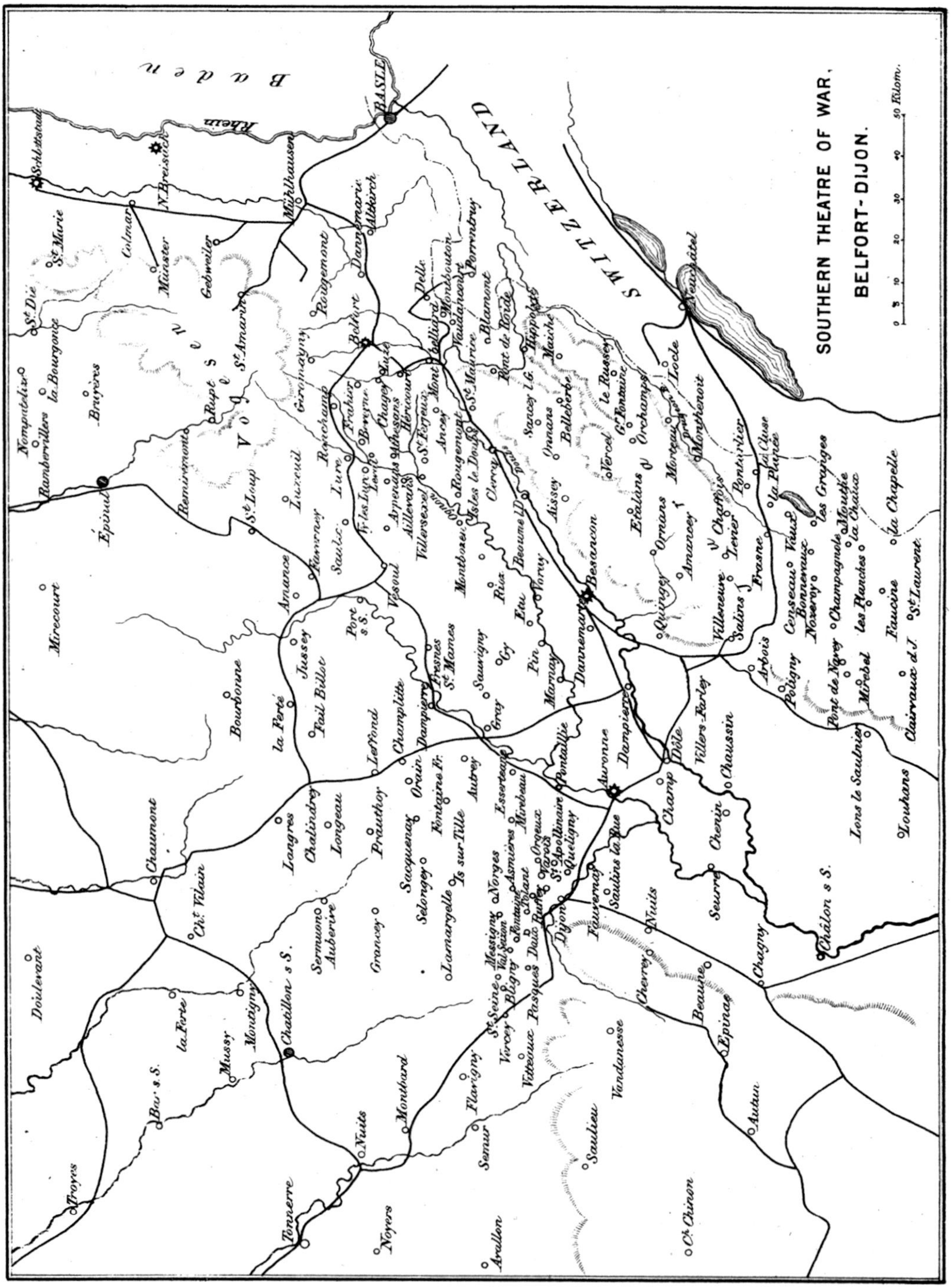

The Southern theatre of war – Belfort, Dijon.

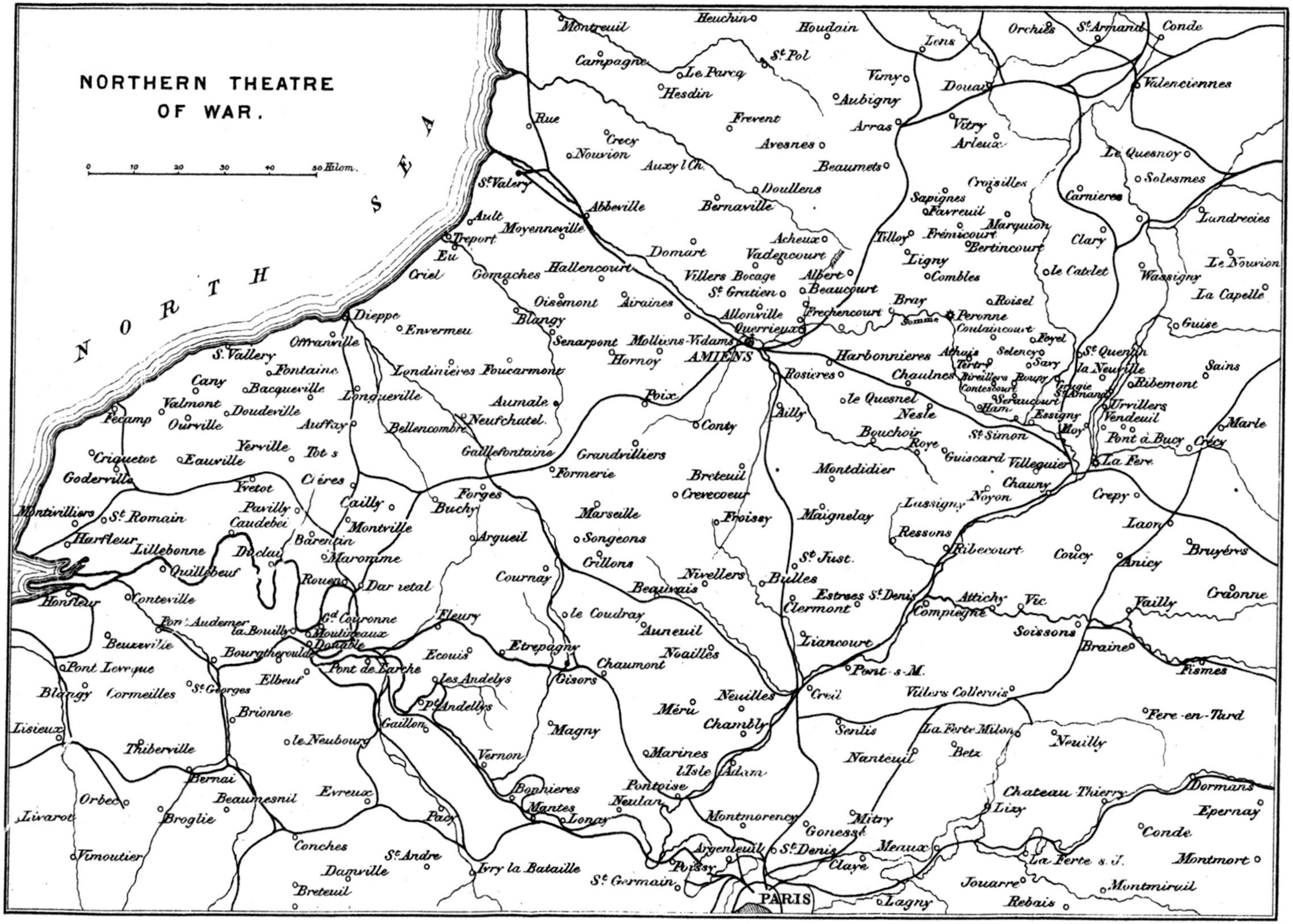

The Northern theatre of war.

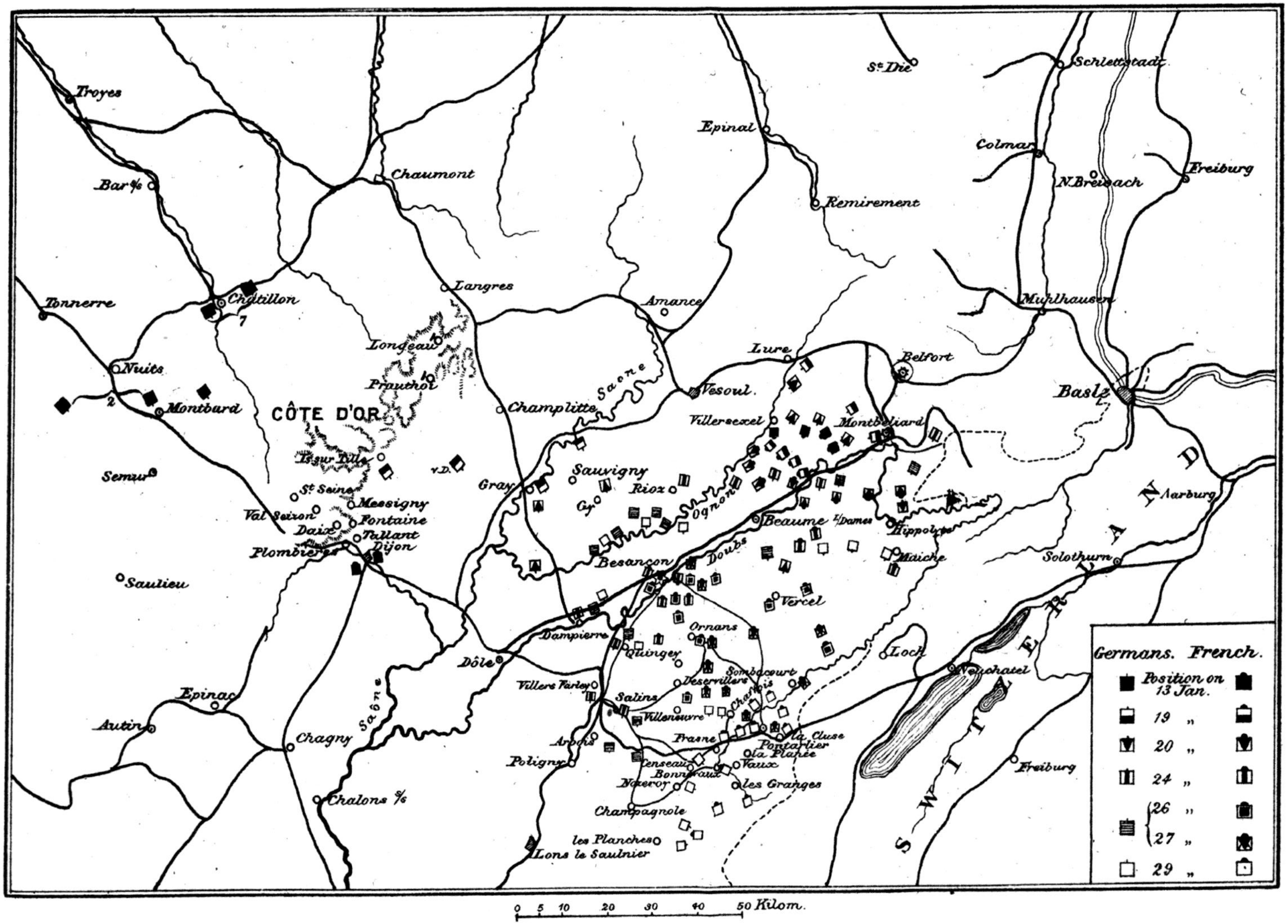

Operations of the Southern Army against Bourbaki.

Chapter 1

Events after the Battle of Sedan

With the result of the fighting at Sedan, Moltke had achieved his goal of neutralising the French imperial army. That part which was not made prisoner was ensconced within the forts of Metz and its commander, Marshal Bazaine, showed little sign of any major aggressive action (although political intrigue was not wanting). The German Second Army of Prince Frederick Charles invested the place to ensure that he did not. The German strategy was to march on Paris as it did in 1815 after the Battle of Waterloo and dictate terms of peace to whoever formed the French government. Who to treat with was still not clear as the Prussian Crown Prince with his army of Prussians and south German troops followed by the Saxon Army Corps made its way to Paris.

In 1866, after the Battle of Königgrätz, Bismarck prevailed upon the king of Prussia to stop the war and open negotiations to prepare for peace. It was a difficult situation with the generals all for continuing hostilities in the flush of victory. After Sedan and Napoleon's surrender, he again argued that the enemy had been defeated and that it made good sense to call a halt and propose peace. Bismarck saw that further military action would be of no consequence and that the French imperial government, under a regency of the empress or the prince imperial, could be brought to the table and forced to concede the loss of Alsace and parts of Lorraine and pay a huge indemnity. This had been the objective of his political manoeuvring since the humbling of Austria. He had no wish to see the French Empire disappear – only its replacement as the major power in Europe by the new Germany. However, this time, the king, Moltke and the General Staff, and all the Prussian generals could not be deflected from their desire to dictate terms in front of or within Paris itself. Long memories of the first Napoleon dictating terms to the Prussian king in Berlin in 1806 had not been forgotten.

Within days of the victory at Sedan, Prussian troops were on the march, after sorting themselves out and making provision for the enormous numbers of French prisoners and the administration of the occupied lands.

By 19 September Paris was surrounded by six German Army Corps forming a barrier 50 miles in circumference – not yet a siege, but an effective blockade, nevertheless. It was not until early January 1871 with the commencement of the bombardment that the siege began in earnest.

The war was far from over, between 4 August and 28 January there were:

156 'significant small actions'
17 major battles
26 fortresses captured
11,650 French officers made prisoner
363,000 French soldiers captured
6,700 artillery pieces taken
120 French eagles or standards in German hands.

Prussian infantry advancing to the attack, note the drummer in the second rank on the far left.

Stores at Cologne railway station for the German army besieging Paris. (*Illustrated London News*)

A Prussian siege battery before Paris. (*The Graphic*)

In addition, over 14,000 men, 12,000 horses, plus artillery and wagons were disarmed on Belgian territory after the Battle of Sedan. On 1 February, nearly 85,000 officers and men crossed the frontier into Switzerland, surrendering 100 artillery pieces and 80,000 rifles to the Swiss authorities.

To give some context, here is a list of events from the Battle of Sedan to the end of the war:

2 September 1870: The French Army surrenders at Sedan and Napoleon is taken prisoner (to the great surprise of the German leaders, Napoleon had not escaped from the city before it was surrounded). At a rough count 104,000 officers and men, 413 artillery pieces and 139 fortress guns fall into German hands. Napoleon is sent to a castle near Kassel where he is kept until freed on 19 March 1871.

4 September 1870: The Second Empire is officially replaced by the Third Republic and a new Government of National Defence is formed in Paris, led by General Trochu and including Leon Gambetta and Jules Favre.

12 September 1870: Adolphe Thiers, a member of the new government, tours Europe attempting to find allies, or mediation. He visits London, Vienna and St Petersburg, without success.

19 September 1870: Paris is cut off from the rest of France and Jules Favre opens discussions with Bismarck with a view to peace. The talks reach no conclusion as the Germans insist on the annexation of Alsace and portions of Lorraine as part of deal, which the French cannot agree to.

28 September 1870: The city of Strasbourg, which had been besieged, surrenders, releasing German troops for operations against French field forces.

7 October 1870: Gambetta, as Minister of the Interior is sent to the seat of the new government outside Paris (initially at Tours on the Loire) to organise the new armies of France. His only means of leaving Paris is by gas-filled balloon. The French Army of the Loire is formed.

Departure of a balloon from Paris at night. (*Illustrated London News*)

THE ILLUSTRATED LONDON NEWS

REGISTERED AT THE GENERAL POST-OFFICE FOR TRANSMISSION ABROAD.

No. 1638.—VOL. LVIII. SATURDAY, FEBRUARY 25, 1871. PRICE FIVEPENCE

Bourbaki's army crosses the Swiss border into internment. Note the Swiss soldier on the left. (*Illustrated London News*)

21 October 1870: A French garrison attacks the Germans at Buzenval, southwest of Paris, and successfully pushes them back in the direction of the Prussian royal headquarters at Versailles. The Germans later retake the lost ground.
28 October 1870: French volunteers and regulars take the village of Le Bourget, north of Paris and situated between the opposing front lines.
27/29 October 1870: The fortress of Metz in eastern France, under siege since 20 August, finally surrenders, and Marshal Bazaine and 120,000 French regular troops, National Guards and volunteers are taken prisoner.
2 November 1870: Germans lay siege to Belfort in Alsace.
24 November 1870: Thionville, near Metz and under siege by the Germans, surrenders.
27 November 1870: The Germans defeat the French Army of the North at Amiens on the Somme.
1–3 December 1870: The French attempt a breakout at Champigny, southwest Paris, with a view to linking up with the Army of the Loire.
2–4 December 1870: The Army of the Loire advances from Orleans towards Paris but is defeated by Bavarian and Prussian troops.
8 December 1870: The French government retires from Tours to Bordeaux. Agreement between the German states leads to the formation of the new German Empire.
17 December 1870: Garibaldi is active in the Dijon area.
3 January 1871: The Battle of Bapaume. The French Army of the North is defeated by the German First Army.
5 January 1871: German artillery begins bombardment of Paris.
18 January 1871: The German Empire is proclaimed, and King William of Prussia becomes Kaiser.
19 January 1871: The Battle of St Quentin. The French give up their intention to relieve Paris. At the second Battle of Buzenval, the French make some gains, but are eventually pushed back into Paris.
20 January 1871: General Trochu seeks peace and hands over command of the Army of Paris to General Vinoy.
22 January 1871: There is rioting in Paris and exchange of gunfire between the *Gardes Mobile* and the *Gardes Nationale.*
23 January 1871: A meeting takes place between Jules Favre and Bismarck to discuss a treaty of peace.
26 January 1871: Favre and Bismarck agree a 21-day armistice.
1 February 1871: The French Army of the East agrees to lay down its arms and be interred in Switzerland.
8 February 1871: Elections are held in France that return a royalist majority (made up of a mix of supporters of Bonapartists, Orleanists and Bourbons).
15 February 1871: The armistice is extended.
18 February 1871: Belfort, still under siege, is ordered to cease resistance.
26 February 1871: Peace preliminaries are signed at Versailles.
1 March 1871: The Germans march into Paris but leave at 11 am on 3 March.
10 March 1871: Adolphe Thiers, now leader of the National Assembly, assembles the new French government at Versailles.
18 March 1871: Citizens of Paris and the National Guard dismiss the plan for peace with the Germans, demanding to uphold the idea of the Republic and rising in revolt.
19 March 1871: Napoleon III is set free and retires to England. The Paris Commune begins. Communes are set up in Lyon and other French cities.
10 May 1871: The Treaty of Frankfort is signed, ending the war.
28 May 1871: Defeat of the Paris Commune.

Later in 1873, Napoleon died in exile, and, on 16 September, the Germans left French territory, the cash penalty demanded by the Treaty of Frankfurt having been paid. In 1875 a government with a Republican

Württemberg Jäger in action at Champigny, late November 1870. (Drawing by Richard Knötel)

The Bavarians at Coulmiers, 9 November 1870.

majority took power in France, ending any further monarchist hopes, which were finally dashed by the death of Napoleon's son, the prince imperial (in Zululand) in 1879.

After Sedan, with the German armies around Paris and the French imperial armies scattered, either prisoners or trapped in fortresses, the war continued as separate campaigns with little cooperation between northern, eastern, and western French armies. Despite Gambetta's best efforts, the difficulties were insuperable. The main objective of these disparate forces was the relief of Paris and the breakup of the several German armies, which, with the proclamation of the king of Prussia as German emperor, now became the forces of Imperial Germany.

France's arguably most competent general, commanding the troops in the north fighting over places whose names would become too familiar during the First World War, had great difficulty welding his few regulars and masses of *Garde Mobiles* into an effective force. Faidherbe was an energetic officer but had little direct contact with the Republican government and the rest of France. When the Paris garrison planned a sortie and needed Faidherbe to coordinate plans, the message was sent by balloon which overshot the areas controlled by friendly troops and even France itself and ended up in Norway. By the time the messages had been collected and redirected, the planned sortie had been repulsed by the German forces without any outside distraction.

Despite the apparent success of the Republican revolution in September 1870, France was not a single political entity and its many of its armies and generals harboured their own ambitions. While the Second Empire seemed discredited, there was still considerable support for the idea of 'Bonapartism' and there remained a possibility that the imperial family, in the person of Empress Eugenie, or the prince imperial, or a successful general acting as regent could resume power. There was also a lingering 'monarchist' faction,

The Volunteers of the West (Légion de Volontaires de l'Ouest) in action, a somewhat romanticised view. (*Illustrated London News*)

French Garde Mobiles on the march. (Drawing by Richard Knötel)

Enrolling volunteers for Garibaldi in the Place de l'Hotel de la Ville, Lyons. (*Illustrated London News*)

and both Bourbons and Orleanists harboured pretenders to the throne. Regional sympathies had their supporters: among members of the new government taking shelter in Bordeaux, the fear of the Army of Brittany being too successful in the field was very real. These undercurrents gave Bismarck a real dilemma – with just whom should he negotiate? The Republicans, especially those in Paris or sitting in Bordeaux, seemed the party not necessarily with the most support, but with the greatest authority and ability to impose their will on the country.

Throughout the autumn and winter of 1870, French armies of considerable size manoeuvred in the north under Faidherbe, the east under Bourbaki, and in the Vosges region following the attempts of Garibaldi to disrupt German communications, as well as the massive offensives in the Loire Valley directed towards Paris. Fortunately, for Moltke and the German plans, these French actions had little or no coordination and were defeated after some hard fighting, especially on the Loire.

Chapter 2

The New French Armies after Sedan

Following the disaster at Sedan the French field armies were either on their way to prisoner of war camps in Germany or huddled round the fortress of Metz, blocked effectively by the German army of Prince Frederick Charles of Prussia.

A French newspaper correspondent observed:

> [T]he number of stragglers was enormous, and I continually met soldiers who did not know where their regiments were. I had seen men and officers disabled by wounds which French soldiers of other days would have despised. I had remarked how untidy and careless the men were allowed to be about their dress and equipment. These things, slight, but significant to a military eye, had caused me, no doubt, some misgivings as to the rapidity of the success we had a right to expect. I saw, also, how prone French officers were to avoid the fatigues of long marches and the discomfort of bivouac. I remember how often I have traversed the French lines at the dead of night and at early dawn, and never heard a challenge, never came across a French vedette, never have fallen in with a party of scouts. On the other hand, I have seen officers spend the time that ought to have been given to their men in cafes or in poor village inns. Often even officers of the staff seemed to neglect their duties for paltry amusements, showing themselves ignorant sometimes even of the name of the department in which they were; so that I have known a French general obliged to ask his way from peasants at the meeting of two roads. I struggled long against all this kind of evidence, but the end is only too clear. Painful it is to me, but I am bound to declare my belief that any further effort France may make can only cause useless bloodshed; and that a means of escape from her peril must now be sought otherwise than by force of arms.[1]

This is a pretty damning observation of the state and morale of the imperial army; the reservists and National Guards were left with little to build upon.

The Importance of Alsace and Lorraine

The new Republican government, however, made the political decision to fight on rather than to come to terms with Bismarck. They knew what the Prussian government's terms would be: an indemnity to pay Prussia for the cost of the war, which would be bad enough, but the cessation of French territory and fortresses in the Alsace and Lorraine regions abutting the German frontiers was politically anathema to

1 Captain Jeannerod, a retired French army officer, who in 1870 was accompanying the army as a correspondent of the newspaper *Temps*.

all in French governing circles. Why did the Prussian king and ministers want to take over these areas, knowing what the French reaction would be? After all, at the end of the earlier war against Austria in 1866 no territory was demanded from her (although huge areas within Germany were added to the Prussian crown), so why the insistence on parts of France?

Alsace and Lorraine had led a chequered existence as a borderland between French and German speakers, sometimes independent, sometimes under French domination, other times under German Hapsburg rule. Under the conditions of the Peace of Ryswick in 1697 the land fell to the French king, Louis XIV. The people, however, were not so sure. As befitted their geographical position their traditions were a mix of the two cultures and their language –Alsatian – was German with French additions. In religion they were Lutheran, which was tolerated in the officially Catholic-dominated France. When the German armies marched through Alsace in July 1870 many country people who spoke the Alsatian dialect welcomed the troops as fellow countrymen.[2]

Rebuilding the French Army

The new government was presented with a dilemma, how to continue the fight. France needed armies to take on the German forces surrounding Paris and Metz, both of which contained large numbers of regular soldiers, organised into battalions, regiments, brigades and divisions. Other German forces took control of the occupied lands between the frontier and Paris and beyond.

The army accompanying the emperor had ceased to exist; 3,200 had been killed, nearly 15,000 wounded and 104,000 made prisoner, with 1,000 wagons and 6,000 horses captured with all the stores and weapons, including 550 guns, falling into German hands. It had been a hard-fought battle – the Germans lost nearly 10,000 men killed, wounded, and missing. France's main field army of over 150,000 men was trapped around the fortress of Metz, so the new government's first task was to find soldiers with which to continue the fight.

France was a rich and populous country, with a population of 38 million containing plenty of young men from the country districts, fit and hardened to manual work, who could be galvanised to join their fellows in the defence of their country. The early part of the war, under the imperial government, had been about invading Prussia, in imitation of the first Napoleon's exploits which resulted in the destruction of the old Prussian army. After Sedan, the focus of the war shifted to the defence of the country from the German invaders. Young men there were in plenty, but they were not soldiers, had no one to lead them (most officers and NCOs were on their way to German prisoner-of-war camps) and they had few arms with which to fight.

The tradition in the French Army, was the ubiquitous '*Système D*' – an official definition of which would be the manner of responding to challenges that requires one to have the ability to think quickly, adapt and improvise when getting a job done. All laudable aims. The letter 'D' refers to a number of French nouns such as *débrouille* (to get by, to sort out). However, in practice it means that 'if you find yourself in a difficult situation that you have not planned for, you will just have to muddle through'! The curse of this system was that, while it could work with intelligent and resourceful officers, it proved disastrous with lazy or

2 The Prussian official position was that those parts of Alsace and Lorraine which had been under 'German' rule in former times should now revert to Germany as a royal province under the king of Prussia. There could be no compromise and military action was the only way to enforce the situation. This remained the case from 1871 to 1918 under German rule; from 1918 to 1940 under French; back to German rule from 1940 to 1945 and thereafter reunification with France.

Titled 'The New Levies of the Republic', this shows, from left to right, troops from Bordeaux, Paris, Tours, the Gironde and a former Papal Zouave. (*The Graphic*)

Calling for recruits in front of the Pantheon, Paris, Autumn 1870. (*Illustrated London News*)

incompetent men or with officers who faced situations beyond their knowledge and capabilities. In 1870 and 1871 too many French officers faced situations where the system left them helpless.

Régiments de Marche and Auxiliary Battalions

Some regular units had escaped the defeat at Sedan and others had evaded the Germans round Metz, but they were hardly enough to challenge even a German division. In areas unoccupied by the Germans former regimental depots retained their support cadres, companies and battalions and squadrons of cavalry. These could be quickly assembled into auxiliary battalions and regiments which were given numbers and designated as '*régiments de marche*' in the new orders of battle. Although some attempt was made to give these new units some cohesion, many were made up of battalions from different parent bodies. Some cavalry units could even be of mixed parentage, squadrons or troops of hussars, *chasseurs* and dragoons making up the numbers. The army in Algeria furnished three regiments of infantry, and troops stationed in Rome to protect the papal territory were recalled. Large numbers of sailors were detached from the now redundant fleet and organised as infantry regiments, perhaps some of the best disciplined and reliable troops of the Republic. The *Gardes Mobile*, intended to support the regular army by laws promulgated in 1868 but mainly in theory, were now activated as a regular fighting force, together with those volunteers fired by patriotic fervour. Battalions of '*Mobiles*' were raised in the provinces and local units were joined together in numbered auxiliary regiments. For example, a battalion was raised in Normandy from each of the districts of Avranches (first battalion), Mortain (second battalion) St Lô (third battalion) and put together as the 30th *Régiment de Marche* in the new 15th Corps. Everyone else was, on paper, ordered into the *Gardes Nationale* which was organised into regiments, also of three battalions, under the title of the 'Mobilised National Guard', nicknamed the 'Moblots'.

French Garde Mobiles of the Seine. (Watercolour by Maurice Toussaint)

French Garde Nationale Mobiles. (Watercolour by Maurice Toussaint)

A list of units of *Mobiles* and their Departments:

1er *Régiment de Mobiles* (Seine)
2e *Régiment de Mobiles* (Seine)
3e *Régiment de Mobiles* (Seine)
4e *Régiment de Mobiles* (Seine)
5e *Régiment de Mobiles* (Seine)
6e *Régiment de Mobiles* (Côtes-du-Nord)

7e *Régiment de Mobiles* (Tarn)
8e *Régiment de Mobiles* (Charentes-Inférieur)
10e *Régiment de Mobiles* (Côte-d'Or)
11e *Régiment de Mobiles* (Loire)
12e *Régiment de Mobiles* (Nièvre)
14e *Régiment de Mobiles* (Yonne)
15e *Régiment de Mobiles* (Calvados)
16e *Régiment de Mobiles* (Rhône)
17e *Régiment de Mobiles* (Aisne)
18e *Régiment de Mobiles* (Charentes)
19e *Régiment de Mobiles* (Cher)
20e *Régiment de Mobiles* (Côtes-du-Nord)
22e *Régiment de Mobiles* (Dordogne)
23e *Régiment de Mobiles* (Finistère)
24e *Régiment de Mobiles* (Haute-Garonne)
25e *Régiment de Mobiles* (Gironde)
26e *Régiment de Mobiles* (Ille-et-Vilaine)
27e *Régiment de Mobiles* (Isère)
28e *Régiment de Mobiles* (Loire-Inférieure)
29e *Régiment de Mobiles* (Maine-et-Loire)
30e *Régiment de Mobiles* (Manche)
31e *Régiment de Mobiles* (Morbihan)
32e *Régiment de Mobiles* (Puy-de-Dôme)
33e *Régiment de Mobiles* (Sarthe)
34e *Régiment de Mobiles* (Deux-Sèvre)
35e *Régiment de Mobiles* (Vendée)
36e *Régiment de Mobiles* (Vienne)
37e *Régiment de Mobiles* (Loiret)
38e *Régiment de Mobiles* (Seine-et-Marne)
39e *Régiment de Mobiles* (Eure)
40e *Régiment de Mobiles* (Ain)
41e *Régiment de Mobiles* (Ardèche)
42e *Régiment de Mobiles* (Aveyron)
43e *Régiment de Mobiles* (Bouches-du-Rhône)
45e *Régiment de Mobiles* (Hérault)
44e *Régiment de Mobiles* (Gard)
46e *Régiment de Mobiles* (Nord)
47e *Régiment de Mobiles* (Nord)
48e *Régiment de Mobiles* (Nord)
49e *Régiment de Mobiles* (Orne)
50e *Régiment de Mobiles* (Seine-Inférieure)
51e *Régiment de Mobiles* (Seine-et-Oise)
52e *Régiment de Mobiles* (Somme)
55e *Régiment de Mobiles* (Jura)
56e *Régiment de Mobiles* (Haute-Marne)
57e *Régiment de Mobiles* (Haute-Saône)
58e *Régiment de Mobiles* (Vosges)
59e *Régiment de Mobiles* (Aube)

61e *Régiment de Mobiles* (Somme, Marne)
62e *Régiment de Mobiles* (Ille-et-Vilaine, Finistère)
63e *Régiment de Mobiles* (Eure-et-Loir)
64e *Régiment de Mobiles* (Aisne, Indre, Puy-de-Dôme)
65e *Régiment de Mobiles* (Rhône)
66e *Régiment de Mobiles* (Mayenne)
67e *Régiment de Mobiles* (Haute-Loire)
68e *Régiment de Mobiles* (Haut-Rhin)
69e *Régiment de Mobiles* (Ariège)
70e *Régiment de Mobiles* (Lot)
71e *Régiment de Mobiles* (Haute-Vienne)
72e *Régiment de Mobiles* (Cantal, Yonne)
73e *Régiment de Mobiles* (Loiret, Isère)
74e *Régiment de Mobiles* (Lot-et-Garonne)
75e *Régiment de Mobiles* (Loir-et-Cher, Maine-et-Loire)
76e *Régiment de Mobiles* (Ain, Aude, Isère)
77e *Régiment de Mobiles* (Tarn, Maine-et-Loire, Allier)
78e *Régiment de Mobiles* (Vendée, Gironde, Lot-et-Garonne)
80e *Régiment de Mobiles* (Deux-Sèvres, Ardèche, Isère)
81e *Régiment de Mobiles* (Charente-Inférieure, Cher, Indre)
82e *Régiment de Mobiles* (Vaucluse, Drôme)
83e *Régiment de Mobiles* (Aude, Gers)
84e *Régiment de Mobiles* (Morbihan, Indre)
85e *Régiment de Mobiles* (Gers, Vienne)
86e *Régiment de Mobiles* (Sâone-et-Loire)
87e *Régiment de Mobiles* (Lozère, Tarn-et-Garonne)
88e *Régiment de Mobiles* (Indre-et-Loire)
89e *Régiment de Mobiles* (Var, Gironde)
90e *Régiment de Mobiles* (Corrèze, Sarthe)
91e *Régiment de Mobiles* (Pas-de-Calais)
92e *Régiment de Mobiles* (Calvados, Manche)
94e *Régiment de Mobiles* (Seine-Inférieure, Marne)
97e *Régiment de Mobiles* (Haute-Savoie)
101e *Régiment de Mobiles* (Somme, Marne)
102e *Régiment de Mobiles* (Nord)
Régiment des Alpes-Maritimes
Régiment de Corse
Régiment de Ardennes

It was not possible, of course, to recruit in those Departments occupied by the German forces. Indeed, the Germans issued an official proclamation that the French government's call for a general mobilisation was to be ignored in areas under their control.

Early in the war, on 28 July 1870, a law was passed authorising the creation of auxiliary regiments (officially called the *régiments de marche*) from the fourth battalions of the regular infantry regiments currently forming the regimental depots. A further law passed on 29 September organised the depot companies of the *chasseur* battalions into new auxiliary *chasseur* battalions. The Roman Legion, which had spent the previous four years supporting the papal government, were established as a six-company battalion on 1 October as the 1st *Infanterie Battaillon de Marche*. A law passed on 2 October established 11 auxiliary infantry

French Garde Mobiles in action. (Watercolour by Maurice Toussaint)

regiments and three auxiliary regiments of zouaves, each of three battalions. Three *chasseur* battalions, each of four companies, were also raised. The same law also authorised an auxiliary regiment of Algerian *tirailleurs* with two battalions of six companies. A law passed on 14 November confirmed the raising of 18 auxiliary infantry regiments, a fourth auxiliary regiment of zouaves, six auxiliary battalions of *chasseurs* and a third battalion for the Algerian *tirailleurs*. A law of 13 December raised 15 auxiliary regiments of infantry, nine auxiliary battalions of *chasseurs*, a disciplinary battalion, and an auxiliary regiment of African light infantry of two battalions. A law of 30 January 1871 ordered a further 16 auxiliary infantry regiments, five battalions of auxiliary *chasseurs* and a second auxiliary regiment of Algerian *tirailleurs* to be raised.

On 16 December 1870 the auxiliary battalions of *chasseurs* which had over 800 men on strength were increased to six companies, with men taken from the line infantry if needed. However, the raising of new units was not always carried out according to the overall plan. From 4 September 1870 until the armistice at the end of January 1871, 56 auxiliary regiments were raised outside of Paris. The auxiliary regiments numbered 29 to 33 were formed with three battalions taken from the eighth (depot) companies of the 3rd battalions of the line infantry.

The Abolition of the Imperial Guard

The new government had, of course, to abide by its Republican principles and on 28 October a decree was passed abolishing the Imperial Guard of Napoleon's Army. The decree ran:

> The Government of National Defence,
> Decrees:
> Art 1. The Imperial Guard is abolished.
> Art. 2. The dismissal will take place as and when circumstances permit. It will take place immediately with regard to those parts in Paris.[3]
> Art. 3. The officers, non-commissioned officers, corporals or brigadiers (in the cavalry) and the soldiers of the ex-Guard, who currently serve in the auxiliary regiments, will receive the pay of their rank and class, as paid to the line, from November 1st.
> Done in Paris, October 28, 1870.

Materiel Shortages

While shortage of manpower seemed to be a problem that could be rectified, there were other more difficult shortages that were to cause problems. Nearly all of France's artillery materiel had been captured, leaving, it was said, but six guns available for use in the whole of the country. The question was, should the existing muzzle-loaders continue to be produced, which had proved to be markedly inferior to the Prussian Krupp guns, or should the new model bronze breech-loader, which had been developed and tested before the outbreak of the war, be introduced? The answer turned out to be both models. Existing facilities could produce the old muzzle-loaders quickly, while new machinery was needed for the breech-loaders (gun factories in Paris were set up to produce the new pieces, but they were only employed in defence of the capital). Hundreds of thousands of Chassepot rifles had been lost or captured so it was not possible to equip all the new armies with this excellent weapon and so an older model rifle[4] was issued in its stead. This weapon was a conversion of a muzzle-loading percussion gun to breech-loading, but it was slower to load and had a poorer performance. The volunteers issued with it were resentful of what they saw as second-class status. The arsenals were cleared and some of the new units had to be satisfied with muzzle-loading percussion rifles until newer weapons were produced or obtained from factories all over France or imported from outside the country. The Prussian leaders

---

3 The new government held direct power in Paris so could implement the decree immediately. Its authority was weaker outside the capital and many members of the Imperial Guard were scattered throughout France as well as prisoners of war in Germany.

4 The converted Model 1822 or 1842 with a moveable breech cover that resembled the lid of a snuff box. Hence the name by which it was referred: the *tabatière*.

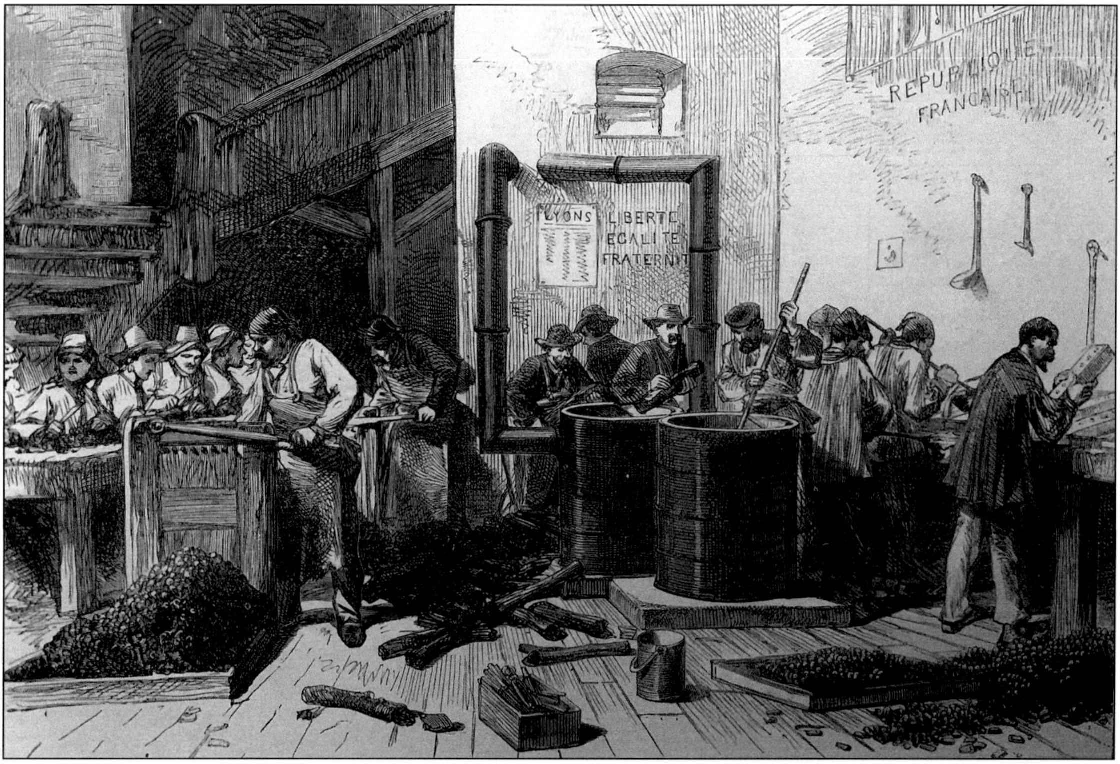

Making Chassepot bullets at Lyons. (*Illustrated London News*)

particularly blamed the United States and England for selling large quantities of arms, which they saw as unnecessarily prolonging the war.

A New French Army

With Paris encircled, the new government established at Tours had to start from scratch building a new military organisation. With all the organs of the state being based in the capital, they had no maps and not even an intelligence department. To make matters worse the politicians were divided amongst themselves as to how to prosecute the war. However, one member of the new government – Leon Gambetta, the Minister of the Interior – having escaped from Paris by balloon, soon galvanised the military authorities by his forceful personality and boundless energy. He also became Minister of War, and his influence put purpose and direction to the conduct of the war thereafter.

The main priority for the French government and its armed forces was to break the German hold on Paris and so all of its energies were bent to this end. With the vast numbers of men now joining the ranks came new problems: how do you turn farm workers, factory hands, shop assistants and so on into soldiers? Who was to train them? Most of the regular officers and NCOs were no longer available so former officers and NCOs and men of education were pressed into service. As well as learning their trade the new troops had to look and feel the part, so uniforms and equipment had to be produced in massive quantities and issued to the men wherever they were based. As well as human flesh, horses were required in enormous numbers to carry cavalrymen, pull guns and haul transport wagons.

THE GRAPHIC

AN ILLUSTRATED WEEKLY NEWSPAPER

VOL. III—No. 60 | Regd. at General Post Office as a Newspaper

SATURDAY, JANUARY 21, 1871

PRICE SIXPENCE | *Or by Post Sixpence Halfpenny*

A night ascent of a balloon, Paris. (*The Graphic*)

The army corps destroyed at Sedan, or incarcerated in Metz (the Guard, the 1st, 2nd, 3rd, 4th, 5th, 6th, 7th, and 12th) were not resurrected, but new corps were raised and formed into regional armies.

Gambetta first sent to North Africa for the return of the regular units stationed there. These consisted of line infantry regiments: the 16th, 38th 39th and 92nd, the Foreign Legion (minus its German elements) of two battalions (60 officers and 1,457 men), three African light infantry battalions and three companies under discipline (that is, soldiers under punishment who had committed some minor crimes not serious enough to be dismissed from the army). This amounted to 429 officers and 13,427 men. Of the sapper companies, Algeria supplied 18 officers and 653 men.

A cavalry division, that of General Reyau, which had escaped the German encirclement at Metz consisted of the 9th Cuirassiers, 6th Dragoons, 2nd and 5th Lancers, 11th *Chasseurs* and the 5th Hussars, also detachments of Algerian *spahis*. In total, 200 officers, 2,300 men and 2,700 horses.

The artillery had seven batteries forming in the provinces with 1,500 men and 1,800 horses, as well as a further five batteries brought from Algeria with 54 officers, 1,807 men and 572 horses.

French Spahi. (*The Graphic*)

Artillery of the Garde Nationale, Paris, during exercises near Notre Dame. (*Illustrated London News*)

Depots

Throughout France every infantry and cavalry unit maintained its regimental or battalion depot. These depots were made up of regular troops who supplied their parent unit with reserves and replacements as required. There were 91 infantry regimental depots, 14 *chasseur* battalion depots, three of zouaves and three of *Turcos*. The number of soldiers totalled 1,274 officers, and 100,472 men. The cavalry had nine depots for the cuirassiers, 11 for the dragoons, eight for the lancers, nine for the *chasseurs*, seven for the hussars and four for the *Chasseurs d'Afrique*, contributing 772 officers, 27,237 men and 13,359 horses. The sapper companies had two depots with 39 officers and 2,012 men. The transport corps had two depots with 37 officers, 4,976 men with 4,383 horses.

The following example of the depot system is based on the 5th Battalion *Chasseurs à Pied*. On 22 July the regular battalion left its depot at Rennes (Brittany) for Thionville (near the border with Luxemburg) with a strength of 23 officers, 584 men and ten horses. On 4 August a further 100 men were sent to Thionville. On 17 August, the 7th Company with three officers and 169 men was sent to Paris. In September, an auxiliary company was formed followed by the 1st and 2nd Depot Companies. At the end of the month, the 8th Company and the 1st Depot Company were sent to Vierzon (south of the Loire near Orleans) to form the 6th Auxiliary Battalion of *Chasseurs à pied* of six officers and 600 men. The 2nd Depot Company at Rennes of two officers and 350 men became part of the 3rd Auxiliary Battalion of *Chasseurs à pied*. The 3rd and 4th Depot Companies formed on 14 October. On 8 November the 5th, 6th, 7th and 8th Depot Companies were formed. A new Auxiliary Battalion, numbered 11, was formed with 13 officers and 1,338 men. On 11 November the 9th, 10th, 11th and 12th Depot Companies were formed and become the 12th Auxiliary Battalion of *Chasseurs à pied* with 15 officers and 964 men. The 13th and 14th Companies were raised as part of the 13th Auxiliary Battalion of *Chasseurs à pied*, with eight officers and 360 men. On 29 November a 15th Company was raised with three officers and 216 men and sent to Lyon to form part of the 21st Auxiliary Battalion of *Chasseurs à pied*. In mid-January two further companies, the 16th and 17th, were raised and sent to Rochefort on the Atlantic coast with six officers and 350 men to form part of the 27th Auxiliary Battalion of *Chasseurs à pied*. On 1 March 1871 the depot consisted of the 3rd Depot Company and an auxiliary company with 11 officers and 281 men.

A further example is the 50th Infantry Regiment. On 1 August, inclusive of its IV Battalion and Depot, there were 17 officers and 820 men in Langres (with a detachment of 14 men at Fort des Rousses and 14 men at Salins). On 8 August, after sending three detachments (1,100 men) to the active battalions, this number was reduced to 325 untrained men, who had uniforms but no equipment, including tents, cooking pots and cartridges. By 15 August, the unit was up to at least 700 men.

Number of Troops

On paper Gambetta could call upon an impressive number of troops for his new armies:

Regular army in France and Algeria: 180,000
Mobile National Guard: 225,000
Class of 1869 incorporated in the Mobile National Guard: 140,000
Class of 1870: 160,000
Free corps volunteers: 30,000
Men aged 25–35 (Law of 10 August): 170,000
Classes 1865 and 1866 (Law of 13 August): 10,000
Grand total: 915,000

The number of trained troops was limited to the regular army, and apart from a few ex-soldiers, the rest were impressive only in their numbers. Training began immediately, consisting of drill without arms, uniforms or equipment. While enthusiasm was not lacking everything else was and the ability to organise the mass into soldiers would take time – the one thing of which Gambetta did not have enough.

Organisation

New situations called for a new organisation. The troops who managed to get back to Paris were initially formed into the recently activated 13th and 14th Army Corps, later reformed into a new organisation under the overall title of the 'Army of Paris'. The first newly formed corps, the 15th, was established in Normandy with the infantry regiments brought from Algeria, including the Foreign Legion. Added to this corps were several *régiments de marche* (that is, the new auxiliary regiments), six *Gardes Mobiles* regiments and a battalion of marine infantry. The cavalry division was that of General Reyau, mentioned above. The infantry brigades were mixed with a regular regiment, an auxiliary regiment of *Gardes Mobiles*, and a regiment or battalion of the mobilised *Garde Nationale*. These latter were not all allocated numbers as the line and auxiliary regiments but carried the title of the Department where they were raised.

The order of battle of the new 15th Corps was constituted as the old imperial corps with three divisions of infantry, one of cavalry with artillery and engineers. However, the troops were a mix of regulars, auxiliary regiments and the mobilised *Garde Nationale*. The difficulty of identifying units was compounded by every new corps having a first, second and third infantry division each of two or more brigades. Thus, there were several first brigades of a first division throughout the Armies of the Republic.

French Fusilier Marines. (Watercolour by Maurice Toussaint)

For example, 15th Corps (as originally organised) consisted of the following:

First Infantry Division
First Brigade: 4th Auxiliary Battalion *Chasseurs*; 38th Line Infantry Regiment; 1st Zouave Regiment; 12th Regiment Mobilised National Guard; 1st Battalion Marine Infantry
Second Brigade: Regiment of Algerian *tirailleurs*; 29th Auxiliary Regiment; 18th Regiment Mobilised National Guard (Charentes)
Artillery: Three batteries, one from each of the 2nd, 6th and 13th Regiments
Engineers: 1st section of the 19th Company of the 3rd Regiment

Second Infantry Division
First Brigade: 5th Auxiliary Battalion *Chasseurs*; 39th Line Infantry Regiment; Foreign Legion Regiment; 25th Regiment Mobilised National Guard (Gironde)
Second Brigade: 2nd Zoaves Regiment; 30th Auxiliary Regiment; 29th Regiment Mobilised National Guard (Maine-et-Loire)
Artillery: Two batteries, one each from the 9th and 12th Regiments; a mixed horse battery from the former Imperial Guard
Engineers: 2nd section of the 19th Company of the 3rd Regiment

Third Infantry Division
First Brigade: 6th Auxiliary Battalion *Chasseurs*; 16th Line Infantry Regiment; 30rd Auxiliary Regiment; 32nd Regiment Mobilised National Guard (Puy-de-Dôme)
Second Brigade: 34th Auxiliary Regiment, 37th Auxiliary Regiment; 69th Regiment Mobilised National Guard (Ariege)
Artillery: Three batteries, one from each of the 7th, 10th and 14th Regiments
Engineers: 1st section of the 19th Company of the 2rd Regiment

Cavalry Division
1st Brigade: 6th Dragoons and 5th Hussars
2nd Brigade: 9th Cuirassiers and 1st Auxiliary Cuirassiers
Two attached Cavalry Brigades: the first with the 2nd and 5th Lancers and the 3rd Auxiliary Dragoon Regiment, and the second with the 11th *Chasseurs à cheval* and the 1st Auxiliary *Chasseurs à cheval*

Reserve Artillery: Eight batteries

A mixed division was later added to the 15th Corps, an infantry brigade with the 31st Auxiliary Regiment, the 22nd Regiment of Mobilised National Guard (Dordogne) and two companies of *Chasseurs à pied* as well as a cavalry brigade of the 1st Auxiliary Hussar Regiment and the 2nd Auxiliary Mounted Mixed Regiment.

This gave the 15th Corps a strength of roughly 50,000 men, an impressive figure with a good stiffening of regular units, but would it be enough to take on the German armies detached from Paris who had the task of keeping them as far away from the capital as possible?[5]

At the outbreak of the war in mid-July 1870, the French Army consisted of the Imperial Guard of 25,000 officers and men, 233,000 infantry, 51,000 cavalry, 33,000 artillery and 23,000 engineers, administration, and Train troops – in all a total of 16,800 officers, 351,000 men and 74,000 horses. On 1 September, during

5 The *Gardes Mobiles* were also raised from districts within each Department.

the Battle of Sedan, which plunged the empire into oblivion, the army stood at 18,000 officers, 580,000 men and 61,000 horses. One month later as Gambetta called for the army to be reorganised, the depots began to fill with men and horses: 126,000 infantry, 44,000 cavalry, 22,000 artillery, 6,800 engineers, 27,000 administration and Train troops – a total of 238,000 men plus 3,000 officers, but only 35,000 horses. By prodigious efforts by the end of February 1871 manpower stood at 951,507 officers and men plus available administration troops. Furthermore, the Class of 1871 and previously exempt married men between 21 and 30 years of age were called up, adding a further 436,168 troops and making an enormous total of 1,387,675 men.

Old Armies: After Sedan

At the end of the empire, only six line regiments of infantry from Africa and Italy remained: the 16th, 35th, 38th, 39th, 42nd and 92nd. The rest of the army was made up of 'marching' regiments made up of four depot battalions from several different regiments. The 28th Auxiliary Regiment, made up of the depot battalions of the former Imperial Guard, distinguished itself during the action at Le Bourget, to the north of Paris, during the siege.

Chasseur battalions (30 in total) varied from four to eight companies.

After the disasters of Frœschwiller, Mars-la-Tour and Sedan, the French cavalry barely existed. The Government of National Defence formed from the regimental depots 40 new regiments: ten cuirassiers, ten dragoons, five lancers, two *chasseurs*, four hussars and ten mixed regiments, each composed of four squadrons. The mixed regiments were composed of different types of mainly light cavalry.

New Armies: The Army of the North

An 'Army of the North' was formed in Normandy with troops that had evaded the German advance on Paris and locally raised *Gardes Mobiles*. Created on 18 November, the Army of the North was composed of 30,000 men and 60 guns. It was at first commanded by Testelin and Farre and Bourbaki, and eventually by General Faidherbe. It was organised into two army corps which were given the numbers 22nd and 23rd.

The German First Army marched against it, defeated it and took Amiens on 27 November; the Germans occupied Rouen on 5 December. Faidherbe attempted to retake Amiens but was defeated at Pont-Noyelles on 23 December. He attacked again in the new year and forced the Germans back on Bapaume on 3 January. He then attempted to march on Paris, but on 19 January he was defeated at Saint-Quentin and had to retreat north.

The Army of the North was decommissioned following the armistice of 28 January 1871.

New Armies: The 1st and 2nd Army of the Loire

The Army of the Loire was formed in October following the decision of Leon Gambetta. It was composed of *francs-tireurs* (volunteer irregulars), provincial *Gardes Mobiles* (territorials), naval forces, zouaves and *tirailleurs* from Algeria, plus regular soldiers in depots and reservists. These diverse units formed the 15th Army Corps. On 10 October, the Army of the Loire was defeated by the Bavarian troops of Von der Thann and had to abandon Orléans on 11 October. Thereupon Gambetta sacked its commander and replaced him with General d'Aurelle de Paladines. The army with 70,000 men and 150 guns was reinforced with the 16th Corps of General Chanzy and the 17th Corps of General de Sonis. Together they beat the Bavarians at Coulmiers in November and retook Orléans. Gambetta reinforced the Army of the Loire with the 18th

French Francs-tireurs de la Presse. (Watercolour by Maurice Toussaint)

Corps (General Billot) and the 20th Corps (General Crouzat). However, this force was badly mauled on 28 November at the Battle of Beaune-la-Rolande and in December at Loigny-Poupry.

After the battle at Loigny the army was split into two parts. The 15th, 18th and 20th Corps became the Army of the East under General Bourbaki and was sent to help the French forces around the city of Belfort. The 16th and 17th Corps under Chanzy became the 2nd Army of the Loire to which were added the 21st Corps of General Jaurès (see colour plate) and those Breton volunteers who were based in the training camp at Conlie. This army was attacked and defeated by the Germans at Le Mans and then remained on the defensive until it was disbanded on 14 March 1871.

New Armies: The Army of Brittany

From the start of the war, 50,000 mobilised Bretons were sent to the Conlie camp (near Le Mans) to receive military instruction and form the Army of Brittany:

> On the initiative of M. de Kératry, who left Paris in a gas balloon, the government of national defence decreed, on October 22, the formation of the Army of Brittany.
>
> This army was to consist, so ran the decree, of those men mobilised from the departments of Brittany and Maine, Mobiles still available in those departments, all the Free Volunteer corps in the West, a few thousand line infantry, a few squadrons of cavalry, some sailors, etc. It had to be from 50 to 60,000 men and could even be more numerous, since the mobilised contingent of the five departments of Brittany was, by itself, 80,000 men.
>
> Its objective was to break through the German lines and relieve Paris. It was to start from Le Mans, resting its right on the left wing of the Army of the Loire, on the other on an army that was to be assembled in Normandy. Finally, it was placed under the command of M. de Kératry, a former officer and deputy for Brest, appointed auxiliary general of division, to whom a credit of 8 millions (of Francs) was opened. It was understood that the army of Brittany would be provided by the State with rapid-fire rifles, long-range cannons, volley guns, etc.

So wrote Doctor Robert Gestin, the former Chief Medical Officer of the Army of Brittany.

In fact, they received very few weapons (and those they did receive were of poor quality) and hardly any military training. They suffered from poor living conditions in the camp and there were deaths from illness.

During the fighting round Le Mans, the Breton troops were put into the line against experienced German troops who were well-armed and better fed. They had no confidence in their Springfield rifles and some of their ammunition turned out to be damaged in transit when it was issued to them. They could not stand before the German attacks and gave way. The army commander, General Chanzy, bitterly criticised the Bretons for the collapse of his defence which forced the withdrawal of his whole army.

Doctor Gestin further states:

> When we ordered the levy of the mobilised, the Bretons responded first. The men were crammed into a muddy camp, often without proper leaders, without a cadre of trained men, without instructors, without weapons. Of what use could these men be, of whom only a few were armed with old rifles? Could they be set against numerous troops, well commanded, well-armed, sure of themselves and accustomed to victory like the German troops? No! They had to be brought back and it is very lucky that we were able to do so in time.
>
> These 50,000 men were therefore of no use to national defence. We can therefore say that the considerable effort made by the Breton country in 1870–71 was useless, that it did not delay the German invasion by a minute, finally, that in a word, it would have been better value if they had been left at home.

A sketch of Breton volunteers from *The Graphic*, autumn 1870. (*The Graphic*)

Bivouac of Garde Mobiles under railway arches in Paris. The graffiti on the wall would suggest these troops are Bretons. (*Illustrated London News*)

> First of all, hardly had the decree of formation of the Army of Brittany been promulgated, when prejudiced advisers inspired in Gambetta an unjust mistrust towards the Bretons, who were represented to him as a danger that they might form a royalist and separatist army. As the press and several municipalities, including that of Rennes, reproached the government for refusing arms to the mobilised troops in the vast Camp of Instruction at Conlie, the prefect of Ille-et-Vilaine replied: 'It is true, but we were wrong to make an army of Bretons. In Tours (i.e., the Government of National Defence), these gentlemen fear that it is an army of Chouans (the name given to the peasants in Brittany who were generally Catholic, royalist and anti-republican).

Although there were still a few thousand Chassepots in the arsenals in the west of France, Kératry's demands to give them to the mobilised Bretons was denied. Most of the rifles were sent to the south, where the mobilised troops had not yet left their homes. Kératry threatened to resign, as it was impossible to overcome the hostile influences.

More Infantry

Companies were created by decree of the 2 September at the rate of two per infantry regiment depot. As eight infantry regimental depots were in places besieged by the Germans on 1 September, only provisional companies organised in the 92 depots were taken into account. These companies had to be commanded by retired, though still able-bodied, officers who would agree to return to service with their old rank. Due to the lack of lieutenants and second lieutenants, they could have a second captain. The numbers of sub-officers and corporals (five sergeants and ten corporals per company) had to be made up with the help of soldiers from the depots.

Organisation of Depots

As soon as he arrived in Tours, General Lefort sent orders to the depots to mobilise the 8th companies of the 3rd battalions of all the infantry regiments. A force of 200 men, officers included, was to be composed as much as possible of former soldiers, soldiers of the second portion of the contingents (that is, those not yet called up) and young soldiers of the Class of 1869.

The cadres of the units composing the depots soon became insufficient to administer and train the men who joined their corps, following the measures taken at the beginning of the war for the increase in numbers. Also, on 21 September, the minister authorised the commanders of the military divisions to create, according to the requirements of the service, additional posts of NCOs, corporals, and brigadiers (cavalry corporals). A few days later, the decree of 23 September created four new company officers in the depots of infantry regiments and two in the depots of *chasseur* battalions. In the infantry regiments, the new companies were to be called 1st, 2nd, 3rd, and 4th Depot Companies; additional companies, apart from the two provisional ones organised on 2 September, would take the numbers 5 and 6. The companies were similarly numbered in the *chasseur* battalions.

These company cadres were, in principle, to consist of a captain, a lieutenant and a second lieutenant. It was forbidden to form a cadre with two lieutenants or two second lieutenants, and vacancies were maintained if it was impossible to fill them in accordance with these requirements. However, the disproportion between the number of candidates for the ranks of captain and lieutenant and the much more numerous NCOs likely to be promoted sub-lieutenants led the Minister of War to decide that in the management of the depot companies not having a lieutenant, there could be two second lieutenants appointed, with the oldest fulfilling the functions of lieutenant and replacing the captain in case of absence.

As of 28 September, two of the cadres trained in the depots of the line each received 200 men, and the minister stressed the speedy formation of these companies and asked to be informed when they were ready to be mobilised.

The constitution of regiments and auxiliary battalions soon removed from the corps depots most of the company officers created by the decree of 23 September. Both to instruct the recruits of the Class of 1870 and to train new troops as necessary, a decree of 20 October prescribed the creation of the number of company officers necessary to reduce to four the number of mobilisable companies of the depots of the regiments of infantry and reduce to two the mobilisable companies of the depots of the *chasseur* battalions.

Despite this measure, new officers were soon needed to continue organising the infantry troops that were to be sent to the field army. Another decree therefore authorised on 26 November the creation in the depots of new company officers. These cadres were to be trained only when the strength of the troops required it, and in any case, in addition to the two provisional companies, the depots of the infantry regiments could not have more than four companies and the depots of more than two *chasseur* battalions.

Under these conditions, the depots of the infantry corps were found to have, by reason of their strength and the number of their companies, the equivalent to a battalion.

To ensure the administration of every company, a decree of 24 November created the position of an adjutant in each of them for the duration of the war.

Formation of New Marching Regiments and Battalions

Similar to the decree of 28 July that authorised the creation of auxiliary regiments with the 4th battalions of infantry regiments, a decree of 29 September provided for the formation in principle of six companies of battalions of *chasseurs*. These corps were commanded by majors.

With the French officers and soldiers returning from Italy after the dismissal of the Roman Legion, a battalion of six companies was organised by a decree of 1 October, under the name of the 1st Battalion of Auxiliary Infantry.

As the constitution of the new army corps demanded, the Minister urgently created the necessary regiments and auxiliary battalions, and a decree of 5 October confirmed the formation of 11 auxiliary infantry regiments, three auxiliary zouave regiments and 11 auxiliary infantry battalions. Each of these regiments consisted of three battalions of six companies: the battalions of *chasseurs* were only four companies. The same decree also provided for the creation of auxiliary infantry battalions forming a unit commanded by a major.

To organise the various detachments of Algerian *tirailleurs* who came to France, a regiment of two battalions of six companies was organised by decree on 2 October.

Decrees on 14 November and 13 December 1870 as well as 30 January 1871 confirmed the formation first of 18 auxiliary infantry regiments, a fourth auxiliary zouave regiment, six auxiliary foot battalions, a third battalion in the auxiliary Algerian *tirailleurs* regiment, and five auxiliary infantry battalions; second of 15 auxiliary infantry regiments, nine auxiliary infantry battalions, an auxiliary discipline rifle battalion and a two-battalion auxiliary African light infantry regiment; and third of 16 regiments of auxiliary infantry, five battalions of auxiliary *Chasseurs à pied* and a second regiment of auxiliary Algerian *tirailleurs*.

On the other hand, a decree dated 16 December 1870 increased to six companies the battalions of auxiliary *chasseurs* whose strength exceeded 800 men.

Unsurprisingly, the organisation of the auxiliary infantry corps was not carried out in accordance with the various decrees. A total of 56 marching infantry regiments were created in the provinces from 4 September until the armistice. The first five (numbers 29 to 33) were formed into three battalions with the 8th companies of the 3rd battalions. The 34th and 35th auxiliary infantry regiments were formed with the 4th battalions available, the first to three and the second to two battalions of six companies. Some 27

Drilling Garde Nationale on the quay at Saint-Malo. (*Illustrated London News*)

auxiliary regiments, bearing numbers 36–46, 48, 49, 51,52, 55, 57–62, 64–66, 70 and 71 formed mostly of 18 companies, with auxiliary companies usually coming from different depots. This made a total of 80 battalions and 464 companies.

Cavalry

Cuirassier Regiments Formed after the Battle of Sedan

The disruption to the French armies even before the debacle of Sedan necessitated some reorganisation. Squadrons were grouped together to form '*régiments de marche*' (auxiliary regiments as in the infantry). Little notice was taken of each regiment's former designation, so the 1st Auxiliary Regiment was made up of squadrons from the former 5th, 6th, 7th and 10th Cuirassiers (in February 1871 becoming the new 1st Regiment); 2nd Auxiliary Regiment from the 1st Cuirassiers, the *cent-gardes*, the Cuirassiers of the Guard and the Carabineers of the Guard (later the 2nd Cuirassiers); the 3rd Auxiliary Regiment from the 2nd, 3rd, 8th and 9th Cuirassiers (later the 3rd Cuirassiers); the 4th Auxiliary Regiment from the 1st, 3rd, 5th and 8th Cuirassiers (later the 4th Cuirassiers); the 5th Auxiliary Regiment from the 6th and 7th Cuirassiers, the Cuirassiers and the Carabineers of the Guard (later the 5th Cuirassiers); the 6th Auxiliary Regiment from the 2nd, 3rd, 4th and 10th Cuirassiers (later the 6th Cuirassiers); the 7th Auxiliary Regiment from the 2nd, 7th and 8th and the Cuirassiers and Carabineers of the Guard (later the 7th Regiment); the 8th Auxiliary Regiment from the 1st, 4th, 5th and 6th (later the 8th Regiment); the old 9th were reformed as the new 9th; the 10th Auxiliary Regiment was formed from the 3rd, 4th, 6th and 9th (later the 10th Cuirassiers); the 11th Auxiliary Regiment was formed from the 5th, 7th and 10th Cuirassiers and Cuirassiers of the Guard

French mixed cavalry from the Republican armies. (Watercolour by Maurice Toussaint)

(later the 11th Cuirassiers); and the 9th Auxiliary Regiment from the 5th, 8th and 10th Cuirassiers and the Cuirassiers of the Guard (later the 12th Cuirassiers).

Auxiliary Cavalry Regiments

The cuirassiers were kept together in their auxiliary regiments, as were many squadrons of medium (dragoons, lancers) and light cavalry (hussars, *chasseurs*), but where circumstances made this impossible new regiments of '*cavalerie mixte*' were formed from the depots and debris of the imperial army. These were primarily light cavalry made up of squadrons of hussars, *chasseurs* and dragoons. The French corps structure was maintained in the new army, with each consisting of two (or sometimes three or even four) infantry divisions with a cavalry division. Each division usually comprised two brigades, each of two regiments. The new mixed regiments – there were at least 11 of them – were scattered around the higher numbered corps: the 2nd and 3rd were part of the 16 Corps; the 4th, 5th and 6th to the 17 Corps; the 8th to the 21 Corps; the 9th and 10th to the 25 Corps; and the 11th ended up in Garibaldi's Army of the Vosges, which also managed to find a squadron of hussars and a squadron of dragoons. The cuirassiers were likewise spread throughout the army: the 1st to the 26th Corps; the 4th to the 17th Corps; the 5th to the 18th Corps; the 6th to the 20th Corps; the 7th to the Loire Army (Column de Tours); the 8th to the 21st Corps; the 9th to the 15th, later the 19th Corps; the 11th to the 26th Corps; and the 12th to the 3rd Army of Paris.

On 28 November 1870, the (French) 18th and 20th Corps, composed mainly of *régiments de marche* and *Gardes Mobiles*, under the command of General Crouzat, were ordered to seize Beaune-la-Rolande, which, along with the surrounding area, was occupied by a large part of the German Xth Corps and covered by numerous outposts. The 20th Corps had to take, almost alone, the weight of the attack as the 18th Corps believed it had to ensure possession of several points before resuming its advance. It was thus stopped in front of Juranville and did not arrive at Beaune-la-Rolande until the end of the battle. This combat delayed the planned march on Paris.

The 5th *Cuirassier de Marche* regiment was responsible for making a movement towards the left of the enemy, which was in reality a diversion to allow the advance of the main body. This regiment, commanded by Lieutenant-Colonel de Brécourt of the carabiniers of the former Imperial Guard, was made up of four squadrons, including one of carabiniers, one of Cuirassiers of the Guard and two of Cuirassiers of the Line. The regiment attracted the attention of the enemy, yet continued to advance, its squadrons in line, under enemy fire, without being hindered by the difficulties of the ground, which was covered with vines, cut by ditches and soaked by recent rains and snow. Most shells sank into the soft earth without exploding. The 3rd Squadron had about ten casualties, of which seven were killed.

The horsemen kept the uniforms of the regiments to which they belonged but removed the imperial insignia. However, the breastplate eagle at this time was not yet removed. The carabiniers retained their scarlet epaulettes and the cuirassiers their white epaulettes. The colonel removed the front crown and the crowned 'N' from his *shabraque*.

Colonel de Brécourt relates that he always had with him 'a *brigadier-trompete* (corporal trumpeter) of the carabiniers and a superior officer of the Cuirassiers of the Line, the latter, taciturn in character'. Colonel de Brécourt subsequently became a major general.

The Volunteer Free Corps, called the *Francs-Tireurs*

Much has been written on the effectiveness of the volunteer units in France after the German victory at Sedan. Some French authors declare that they were a major thorn in the side of the advancing and occupying German armies, while other, German, sources declare them to be merely an annoyance in some areas. The truth probably lies somewhere between the two opposing views at different times and in different locations. Some units acting on their own initiative could be very effective at destroying railways and making some areas dangerous for small parties of German soldiers. Where the French authorities tried to incorporate volunteer units into the field armies, as they did with the Armies of the Loire, they proved more of a hindrance than a military asset. There were always exceptions and Count Lipowski, a former French officer who volunteered his services, led several volunteer units with some success. He defended the town of Chateaudun, delaying the German advance, and led a raid against an enemy cavalry detachment capturing 70 men and 200 horses.

The Germans termed all 'partisans' in the areas they occupied after August 1870 '*francs-tireurs*', be they armed civilians taking pot-shots from windows in towns and villages or from behind trees in the forests, or armed and uniformed units acting (sometimes) as auxiliaries to the French regular army. The rules of conduct authorised the German authorities to deal with civilians caught with 'guns in their hands' harshly, by court martial and the penalty of execution. Propaganda made much of this, but incidents of such extreme measures are difficult to find. Indeed, the Germans prided themselves as acting correctly within the then understood rules.

The political situation concerning Napoleon's dealings with Bismarck in 1867 over the future of Luxembourg (Napoleon wanted 'compensation' for his remaining neutral in Prussia's war with Austria in 1866) generated a rising of patriotic fervour in France. One result was the formation of a number of shooting or rifle clubs, especially in eastern France, which was the most likely area of conflict between the two countries. These clubs organised themselves at their own expense, designed their own uniforms, chose their own officers and NCOs, provided their own arms and equipment and even undertook military training. They were all volunteers and probably joined together for social reasons as much as for patriotic ones.

Many clubs proudly called themselves '*francs-tireurs*' and later in the war they were given official status within the French armed forces as the government tried to exercise some direct control over them. The first company of *francs-tireurs* was formed by a decree of 11 July 1868: the *Francs-tireurs de Colmar*. At the outbreak of the war, they took part in military operations in Alsace and the Vosges and were the only *franc-tireur* corps to carry out an offensive operation across the Rhine into Baden territory in August 1870.

The uniform they chose was similar that of the *Gardes Mobiles*, with slightly different colours: a double-breasted blue tunic with pointed cuffs piped red, shoulder straps also piped red, grey trousers with red stripes, round grey cap with a red band and a red flannel cummerbund. They were armed with a Chassepot rifle and yatagan bayonet.

A typical urban *franc-tireur* unit (raised at Neuilly sur Marne, to the east of Paris), as recorded by a French officer, listed the following professions of its members:

> a commercial traveller, two entrepreneurs, an agent-voyer [road surveyor], a student, four solicitor's clerks, a photographer, nine house painters, six hairdressers, a stonemason, six watchmakers, two cloth printers, two tinsmiths, a gardener, a carpenter, a wood worker, three butchers, two plumbers, five launderers, a blacksmith, a packer, an omnibus coachman, two roofers, three bakers, two wheelwrights, two weavers, a paper-maker, eight labourers, five mechanics, a tanner, a paver, three clerks, a locksmith, a jeweller, a shoemaker, a trimmer, a purse dealer and finally a gymnast.[6]

Age was no bar to recruitment either: the 60-year-old captain of one unit had a retired judge of over 70 and a 12-year-old boy in the same company. Women also joined local units, either in the traditional roles of nursing or as *cantinières*, but some carried a gun and fought in the ranks, and it is even recorded that a few became officers.

---

6 Comte René de Belleval, *Journal d'un capitaine de francs-tireurs* (Paris: Lachaud, 1872).

The government (first the imperial, later the Republican) tried immediately to exercise some control over the free corps volunteers by making a list of those units that were registered with the government, and in early October a report was issued with specific proposals on their organisation and terms of service.

Records collected after 16 September gave the following numbers in the provinces: 302 battalions, companies or free corps, altogether 1,347 officers and 44,245 men; 12 mounted squadrons and 18 platoons altogether 72 officers and 1,530 men; six batteries with six officers and 312 men (one wonders where they got hold of artillery pieces?); and 12 companies or detachments of engineers with 44 officers and 1,043 men. This makes a total: of 1,469 officers and 56,130 men.

The units, however, gave themselves various titles and had varied compliments. The Companies of Charente (Cognac) and Domfront numbered one or two officers and 21 men; the Company of *Tirailleurs* of Toulon had four officers and 150 men; the company of La Roche-sur-Yon, 11 officers and 500 men; but, on the other hand, the Battalion of the Volunteers of Orleans had only six officers and 120 men. At the armistice, further units were in the course of being formed, including 47 battalions, companies or corps comprising 186 officers and 5,108 men, 11 cavalry platoons of 15 officers and 339 men, two companies and one engineer detachment comprising four officers and 126 men.

By order of the Minister of War all corps of volunteers had to be attached to an army corps in the field, or, failing that, to a territorial military division; it was then required to operate in accordance with the orders of the corps commander or the division commander. The volunteers in field at the time of the promulgation of the decree were automatically assigned to the army corps or to the military divisions on the territory of which they were operating and were to make themselves known immediately to the general-in-chief. They could, however, send the minister a request to receive another destination within five days. Failing to comply with these prescriptions, the units were to be disarmed and dissolved.

Francs-Tireurs in the Forest of Orleans. (*The Graphic*)

Sadly, some of the volunteers continued to terrorise the local populations with their misbehaviour and often misconduct. To put an end to these disorders, the minister ordered on 5 January that the malefactors who claimed to be members of a volunteer free corps be brought before the military authority as individuals or in groups to justify their position. Those who belonged to a free corps attached to an army corps would be sent to their headquarters and brought before a court martial. If they could not prove their membership of a recognised unit, they would be drafted into the *Gardes Mobiles* or regular army according to their age.

A notice of 12 September addressed the problem of the volunteer corps. Despite the numerous requests addressed to it, the government would no longer grant new authorisations for the formation of free corps as it was essential to ensure that the mobile and sedentary national guards received all the new model weapons still available. The government recalled 'moreover that the ranks of the mobile national guard and the sedentary national guard remained open to all volunteers, regardless of the faculty which remained acquired to them to enlist for the duration of the war in a corps of regular troop'. The overall numbers of volunteer corps, including those in Paris, ended up forming a total of 2,893 officers and 69,182 troops, divided into 91 battalions, 450 corps forming companies, 28 squadrons, 18 separate mounted platoons and 31 batteries.

However, a battalion of ten companies, together comprising 25 officers and 742 men, was formed from the 4th to the 16th of September (*Francs-tireurs de la Marne*, 11 September; two companies of *Francs-tireurs du Haut-Rhin*, 12 September; *francs-tireurs* from the city of Rouen, 12 September; an Alsatian *franc-tireur* corps formed in Paris on 14 September and sent to Belfort on 26 September; further companies of *Francs-tireurs du Haut-Rhin*, called '*Montagnards*', 14 September; *Francs-tireurs du Midi* or Legion of Provence, 15 September). A company of engineers, the *Ouvriers du Haut-Rhin*, was also organised on 12 September.

Furthermore, the volunteers attached to the 16th Corps (*francs-tireurs* of the Sarthe, of the Gironde, of Constantine, of Saint-Denis) operated in late November in the region of Patay, under the command of Colonel Lipowski, commander of the *Francs-tireurs du Paris*. Colonel Lipowski also had half of the 3rd Squadron of the 1st Auxiliary Mixed Regiment of cavalry and two sections of the 2nd Mountain Battery of the 8th Artillery. Later, on 14 January 1871, the Minister of the Interior and of War decided that in future companies of volunteers would no longer be formed. At the time, the Prefects were ordered to immediately identify those bodies whose organisation was sufficiently advanced to be handed over to the military authorities at short notice. As for the others, their training was halted, and the few volunteers who were still members of those units were dismissed or transferred to the active army or the auxiliary army.

Gambetta eventually decided to incorporate the volunteer corps into the regular Armies of the Loire and the East.

> The delegation of the Government of National Defence, considering that there cannot exist on the territory of the Republic any armed force which is not subordinated to a regular power; given that the operations of the *francs-tireurs* must, in order to combine usefully with those of the other armies, be directed by the military authority, decrees [that] the companies of *francs-tireurs* will be placed at the disposal of the Minister of War and subject, from the point of view of discipline, to the same regime as the Mobile National Guard.

During the armistice, the Government of National Defence resolved to control the units of volunteers more securely. An order of 5 February 1871 decreed that the troops commanded by Generals de Charette and Lipowski and by Colonel de Cathelineau, which, with a few mobile and mobilised units, mainly consisted of volunteers, would be formed into three brigades as part of the 2nd Army of the Loire at Le Mans.

Volunteers of the West

The French withdrew their garrison from Rome at the start of the war and the 'Legion of Antibes' was included in the new corps being mobilised. There were, however, other Frenchmen under arms in Italy whose position was problematic.

The Papal Zouaves were formed as the Volunteer Company of Franco-Belgian *Tirailleurs* in 1860 during a major reorganisation of the papal forces. The strength of the unit was increased to an eight-company battalion on amalgamation with another volunteer unit, the Crusaders of Cathelineau. The battalion received the name of 'Papal Zouaves' on 1 January 1861. The commanders were Colonel Eugene-Joseph Allet and Lieutenant-Colonel Athanase de Charette.

On New Year's Day 1870, the Papal Zouaves formed a regiment of four battalions, composed of six companies each, and of a depot battalion of four companies, together with a company called '*La campagnie hors range*', composed of officers' servants, the tailors, shoemakers and armourers, and the bandsmen and *Sapeurs* of the regiment.

The numerical strength of the different companies varied and, as new recruits arrived and old soldiers left, the same company would vary in its strength at different periods. About 100 men was the supposed complement of each company, but often it was 60 or even less, while occasionally the numbers increased immensely. At the time of the taking of Rome by Victor Emmanuel's troops, the 5th Company, 3rd Battalion, numbered nearly 150 men. At the beginning of 1870, the corps numbered about 3,500 men in all. Of these the most numerous nationalities were Dutch, then French, and after these Belgian, Canadian, English and Irish, Swiss, German and Italian. Spain, Portugal and many other nations sent their representatives, including three or four Africans and one Chinese.

As all the orders and words of command were in French, the majority of the officers were French.

Each battalion was under the command of a commandant, and each had a captain-adjutant-major, nearly corresponding to the adjutant in the English Army, and an adjutant corresponding to an English sergeant-major, and who, like the latter, carried a sword and wore a uniform very like that of an officer, was only ranked as a *sous-officier*, or non- commissioned officer.

Each company had three officers: a captain, a lieutenant, and a sub-lieutenant. Under these were the sergeant-major; the *sergeant-fourrier*, an assistant to the sergeant-major; four common sergeants; and one *sergeant du tir*, to look after the rifles and ammunition of the company. Also, there were eight full corporals, and a certain number of '*fonctionnaires*' or lance-corporals. One corporal, or *fonctionnaire*, was always named '*caporal d'ordinaire*' and his duty was to superintend the buying of meat and so on and the cooking of the food for each company.

The men of the band were under the immediate supervision of a *chef de musique*, with the rank of lieutenant, and a *sous-clief de musique*, along with a sergeant-major, sergeants and corporals of the band. *Le capitaine tresorier*, a captain especially appointed for the purpose, aided by his staff of clerks, composed of a sub-lieutenant, two sergeants, four corporals and some privates, received the money from the intendant of the division. This, every five days, was given out to each sergeant-major, who in turn divided it among the corporals of his company, who in their turn paid it to the men of their squads. The ordinary pay of the private soldier was three sous per day, which could be increased to six sous per day and further increased by promotion.

A total of 1,500 Papal Zouaves took part at the successful Battle of Mentana, fought on 3 November 1867 between French and papal troops against Italian volunteers led by Giuseppe Garibaldi. (An ironic case in point, the ex-Papal Zouaves and Garibaldi's Red Shirts ended up fighting on the same side for the French Republican government against the Germans.)

The Zouaves also fought in the final engagements against the forces of the newly united Kingdom of Italy in September 1870, in which the papal forces were outnumbered almost seven to one. Preparations

French Volunteers of the West, a unit formed primarily from former Papal Zouaves. (Painting by Lionel Royer)

A Volunteer of the West. (Watercolour by Maurice Toussaint)

were being made for a counterattack against the Italians before being told of the surrender by messengers from the pope.

After the capture of Rome by the Italian Army in 1870, the papal army was disbanded and 760 French nationals of the now defunct Papal Zouaves, led by Colonel de Charette, offered the French Government of National Defence their services. They were renamed the '*Légion de Volontaires de l'Ouest*' (Legion of the Volunteers of the West) and by 7 October 1870, the contingent, now augmented by new volunteers and composed of 64 officers, 1,620 men, 80 cavalry and 80 artillerymen, was organised into three six-company battalions, plus three depot companies; a squadron of mounted scouts; and a mountain battery.

The Legion was later reorganised into two battalions with a total of 1,800 men. The 2nd Battalion suffered heavily at the Battle at Loigny, losing 18 officers and 198 men out of a total of 300. The regiment was disbanded in August 1871.

The uniforms worn by the Legion were those of the ex-Papal Zouaves. This was similar to a typical North African zouave costume of a short open jacket over a gilet, with wide trousers, gaiters and black shoes. Headgear was a kepi with a coloured band and piping and a brass hunting horn badge. For historical reasons the uniform colours of officers and men differed. The Papal Zouaves were initially to be dressed in pale blue cloth with black lace and officers naturally ordered their tailors to make up this uniform. However, when the papal treasury found out the price of dressing the men they baulked at the cost and instead ordered the same style but in cheaper grey cloth with red wool lace. This tradition continued throughout the life of the regiment and was carried on when the volunteers reached France. The 2nd Battalion particularly had to be supplied with local, medium quality French cloth known as 'Le Mans' in a pale grey colour. A second batch of a darker grey-blue cloth was supplied from Nantes. The jacket was edged in red wool, including the pointed cuffs and around the false pockets on the front. At the back of the cuffs a strip of red braid was decorated with a dozen small yellow metal buttons. The full trousers had red piping on the outside seems and around the pockets. The gilet also had red wool lace round the neck and down the front. The kepi was in the grey cloth with a red band and red piping around the crown. The front of the red band was decorated with a brass hunting horn; examples show the bell facing to the left for volunteers or the right for NCOs. White or black gaiters were worn as were a black leather equipment pouch and a belt with an open brass buckle. They were issued with Chassepot rifles, but there is also a reference to their having Remington rifles, presumably having brought with them from Italy. Tenders were offered to local suppliers for uniforms for the new volunteers who swelled the numbers of the original contingent. However, it seems that only a description of the uniform was given, rather than an actual pattern as a surviving example shows a typical 'zouave' jacket with red braid in the style of the regular army zouaves looping around a false pocket.

Officers had a similar style of uniform, but of pale blue cloth decorated with black silk lace and piping and with a black velvet band on the kepi. The back of the jacket was further decorated with an intricate black lace design. The officer's gilet had a row of gilt false buttons down the front as did that of the adjutant NCO. Both officers and volunteers had a winter duffel coat, double-breasted with two rows of four yellow metal buttons. The coat had a red lining and was fitted with a hood. Officers wore white gloves and all ranks had woollen gloves – pale blue for officers and grey for the volunteers. Officers were armed with the French infantry officer's straight sword with a black strap and gold tassel. Black leather boots were worn. All ranks used the red waist sash worn under the belt.

Rank was shown by two inverted red wool chevrons above the cuffs for a corporal and a gold chevron for a sergeant. Officers had gold Hungarian knots above the cuffs, or bands of gold lace, with a gilt hunting horn on the kepi, decorated with sequins.

The Legion did not carry a French infantry standard, but a special banner which hung from a crossbar attached to a staff. It was made by the nuns of the abbey at Paray-le-Monial with the reverse worked by the Carmelite nuns at Tours. The swallow-tailed silk sheet displayed, on the obverse, a red sacred heart with gold flames and a green 'crown of thorns' with, above the heart in red, 'COEUR DE JESUS' and below, 'SAUVEZ LA FRANCE'. On the reverse also in red was 'SAINT MARTIN / PATRON / DE LA

FRANCE / PRIEZ / POUR NOUS'. The sheet had a gold fringe and tassels. Above the banner was a white cravat decorated with a red cross and with a gold fringe.

Legion Mounted Scouts

The mounted scouts were raised in France from volunteers, the officers coming from Frenchmen formerly of the papal dragoons. In keeping with their origins, the uniform adopted by the unit closely resembled that of their forebears. They adopted a green double-breasted tunic with two rows of six yellow metal buttons. It had a turn-down collar just revealing the top of the white shirt. The collar and pointed cuffs were piped in red. The back skirts of the tunic were also piped red, with a row of three yellow metal buttons on either side. The front of the collar had a red woollen hunting horn badge. Trousers were blue grey with a wide red stripe on the outside seam. Black leather false boots nearly reaching the knee were worn, along with steel spurs. The troopers were armed with the Chassepot carbine (although another source suggests that they were issued with American Spencer carbines) and the light cavalry sabre Model 1822 with a white wool sword knot. The standard kepi had a green body, piped red and a red band with a green cloth hunting horn badge, black leather peak and chinstrap.

NCOs were distinguished by gold lace inverted chevrons above the cuffs and a gilt hunting horn badge on the collar front and the kepi.

Officers had a uniform in similar colours, with the hunting horn badge on the collars and kepi in gilt, as was the lace rank indication over the cuffs, several rows of Hungarians knots and gold piping on the kepi. Blue-grey riding trousers with a red stripe and black riding boots were worn. Officers also had a calf-length coat, single-breasted with a single row of six gilt buttons and gold lace round the cuffs to indicate rank. The coat had a slanting pocket over each hip. Gloves were brown leather. Officers had a light cavalry sabre similar to that of the troopers with a black silk sword knot with a gold knot.

Medals Worn by ex-Papal Troops

Many of the volunteers who came from Rome had seen action on behalf of the papal regime and had been presented with medals to commemorate their actions. The most common were the Medal for the Battle of Castelfidardo, fought on 18 September 1860, which was a silver open disc hung on a red ribbon with two white stripes edged in yellow; the Medal for the Battle of Mentana of 14 November 1867, which was a silver *cross pattée* hung on a white ribbon with two pale blue stripes. There was also a silver medal hung on a white/ yellow ribbon awarded for good service. Some officers had received a papal order of knighthood – the Order of St Gregory the Great – which was a red enamel eight-pointed star, edged gold and worn on the left breast for a Knight and round the neck on a red ribbon edged yellow for a Knight Commander.

Custom Officers

In France the corps of customs officers had always been semi-militarised, just like the Fire Service and the *Gendarmerie*. In 1823 customs officers in the Pyrenees were mobilised against Spanish Liberal forces that had been spilling over the frontier during the uprising against the monarchy. Customs officers held a special place in France: during medieval times they were important in the collection of customs duties and the prevention of smuggling. Even after the formation of the nation-state called France, there were external and internal boundaries that required a strong police force. In 1831 and 1832 King Louis-Philippe created the military Customs Corps formed on the model of the light infantry with companies and battalions largely composed of retired soldiers. They were under the jurisdiction of the Ministry of Finance during peace-time, but in the event of invasion or war on the borders they were handed over to the Ministry of War. The borders consisted of 'Customs Inspections' which formed a battalion, each made up of several companies under a captain.

During the first month of the war, the imperial government placed the customs officers of 40 *Departments* at the disposal of the Minister of War. On 4 September, out of the 15 battalions formed before the fall of the empire, 14 were in areas occupied by the Germans and only one – the 4th Battalion of the 2nd Eastern Legion – was available and so was assigned to the defence of Belfort. The Government of National Defence continued as far as possible the policy of the empire and raised three more battalions and a company of mobilised customs officers. One company, the *Compagnie des Ardennes*, took part in the defence of Mézières. As for the three battalions, they were incorporated into the field armies.

The customs officers of Valenciennes formed, on 30 August, a battalion with three companies comprising, respectively, 58, 54 and 47 men. On 11 October, a company of 128 men was organised in Dunkirk. On the other hand, the Lille customs officers formed a company of 115 men. The three groups met at Avesnes on 2 November and formed a single battalion of three companies, comprising 11 officers and 402 men. There were five companies in the Calvados (Normandy) battalion.

The customs officers were armed and equipped as the infantry of the line since 1827 so the distinctive colour of the uniform was green, jacket and trousers. The trousers were later changed to a blueish grey with green piping. In 1835 a tailcoat was introduced, also in green, with sky-blue trousers (blue cloth with white threads) piped in madder red. In 1840 officers had silver piping on the trousers: 22.5 mm for lieutenants, 27 mm for captains and 31 mm for senior officers. In 1845, in correspondence with the infantry, a single-breasted tunic was introduced which when closed had a row of nine tin buttons with madder red piping to the collar as well as the green pointed cuffs and down the front of the tunic. The shoulder straps were red. The blue trousers had a 40 mm wide madder red stripe in place of the piping. Belts and straps were black leather. The belt was closed by a large brass buckle, which some illustrations show the word 'DOUANE' marked on it. For full dress a black felt shako was worn with leather peak and chin strap. It had red cloth binding around the top and on each side with a double red pompon at the front. Below this was a tricolour cockade and brass plate. White gloves were worn. For undress a kepi with a green base and blue top with red piping was worn and the blue trousers were tucked into white gaiters. Arms were a Chassepot rifle and bayonet. Traditionally, the customs officers carried a short infantry sabre from their inception and continued to do so instead of the sidearm adopted by the line infantry. It had a brass hilt with a single bar handguard and was carried in a black leather scabbard with brass chape.

NCOs had silver chevrons above the cuffs.

Officers wore a similar uniform, but with silver cord shoulder straps, silver lace on the collar and rank denoted by silver threads above the cuffs arranged in a series of 'Hungarian' knots. The full-dress shako had silver binding instead of red. This uniform was worn until 1872 when a double-breasted tunic was introduced.

Gendarmerie

As well as the regular military forces of the country, France possessed (and still does) a semi-militarised police force, the *Gendarmerie*, which operated outside the cities. Every division of the army had a detachment of *Gendarmerie* who were responsible for discipline and order within their respective units. The government did not ignore this potential resource and even before the fall of the Second Empire, the *Gendarmerie* had been called upon to provide, apart from its provost duties, an infantry regiment with two battalions of six companies and a mounted regiment with six squadrons. These two corps, formed on 15 August in Versailles, were part of the Paris garrison. All members of the *Gendarmerie* who retired on Paris as the German armies advanced were formed into a second mounted regiment and a third battalion of infantry.

The Government of National Defence ordered three main measures in the provinces: first, the creation of auxiliary regiments; second, the mobilisation of the sedentary (local) *Gendarmerie*; and third, the institution of provisional *Gendarmerie* brigades.

French Gendarme. (Watercolour by Maurice Toussaint)

By a decree of 6 October, the government dismissed the elite *Gendarmerie* squadron of the Imperial Guard which had been formed for the security of the imperial residences and the crown forests. The officers, NCOs, corporals and *gendarmes* were transferred to the departmental *Gendarmerie.*

The function of the *Gendarmerie* was independent of the armed forces, which in the field the formations set up in the provinces included, on average per division, an officer, 20 foot *gendarmes* and ten mounted *gendarmes.*

The auxiliary regiments were created by decree on 31 October with men drawn from the *Gendarmerie* legions throughout the country and formed into two mounted regiments, numbered 1 and 2, with each mounted regiment consisting of 480 mounted men divided into four squadrons of 120 men each and one foot regiment, each commanded by a lieutenant-colonel.

The composition of the mounted regiments was set as: staff of one lieutenant-colonel commander, one squadron commander second-in-command, two squadron leaders, two adjutant-majors ranked as captains, one paymaster, one medical officer second class, one aide-major first class, one veterinarian first or second class, one veterinary assistant, two warrant officers and one trumpet corporal, making a total of 14.

Each squadron comprised: one captain, one lieutenant, two second lieutenants, one sergeant-major, six sergeants, one quartermaster, 12 corporals, two trumpeters, two sappers, 96 mounted *gendarmes,* and 20 unmounted *gendarmes,* making a total of 144. The four squadrons together had 576 men and the total strength of a mounted regiment was 590.

Once the regiments were formed, the corps commanders were authorised to fill any vacant officer posts from the NCOs and corporals. Appointments were made on the colonel's proposal, sanctioned by the general commanding the army corps, but were not finalised until they had been approved by of the Minister of War. Trumpeters and sappers were taken from line cavalry regiments.

The infantry regiment comprised 1,200 men divided into two battalions with four companies of 150 men (officers excepted). The composition of this regiment was as follows. Staff: one lieutenant-colonel commander, one battalion commander second in command, two battalion chiefs, two captain-adjutant-majors, one paymaster, one medical officer second class, one aide-major first class, two warrant officers, and one corporal drummer, making a total of 12. Each company: one captain, two lieutenants or sub-lieutenants, one sergeant-major, one quartermaster, four sergeants, eight corporals, two drummers and 134 *gendarmes,* making a total of 153. In all, eight companies, comprised of 1,224 men, meant the total for a regiment was 1,236.

Apart from these three regiments, there were, in the Army of the North, two squadrons of *Gendarmerie* formed in Lille, on 9 November 1870, from *gendarmes* of the 3rd Legion with six officers and 108 men. Also, in the reserve division of the 2nd Army of the Loire, there was a company of *gendarmes* from the Sarthe with three officers and 89 men.

The uniforms worn by the foot and mounted units of the *Gendarmerie* was similar. Both wore a single-breasted blue *habit* with red turnback tails. On the tails was a white grenade badge. The *habit* had a plain blue collar, and the blue round cuffs and cuff flaps were piped in red, as was the front of the garment. It was closed by nine white metal buttons, three buttons on each cuff flap, two at the small of the back and three on each false pocket flap. White shoulder straps on a blue backing ending in a trefoil knot, with, falling from the left shoulder, a white aiguilette, hooked to the upper buttons on the habit. Mid-blue trousers with black lace down the outside seams were worn. There were black shoes for troops on foot and knee-length cuffed riding boots for mounted troops. In full dress a black bicorne hat bound with white lace and a white loop over the tricolour cockade was worn. The sidearm and cartridge box were carried on cross-belts of buff leather edged white. Mounted troops had a single shoulder belt over the left shoulder carrying the cartridge box. Foot troops were armed with a model 1866 Chassepot carbine. The mounted troops were equipped with an 1822 light cavalry sabre with a white sword knot carried on a buff, edged white waist belt closed with a brass buckle embossed with a bursting grenade. NCOs carried silver inverted chevrons above the round cuffs and the aiguilettes were mixed silver and blue cords. In full dress all ranks wore gloves: white for foot troops and light buff for mounted. In service dress all *gendarmes* wore a kepi with a dark blue base and a mid-blue top divided by white lace, the crown was decorated with white piping. A small white grenade badge was fixed to the front of the dark blue band. In the field the foot troops wore black belts.

Forest Wardens/Guards

A Royal Order of 27 August 1831 created companies of forest guides or guards in the 29 departments closest to the borders. Similar to the customs officers, the forest wardens or guards were under the civil authority of the Minister of Finance, but in the event of an invasion of their territory, the companies of the forest guards were to be made available to the Ministry of War. If the men could not return to their homes after the emergency, they would be assigned to a fortified place designated in advance where they would form part of the garrison, so ran the instruction, whether this was ever carried out is questionable.

The imperial government mobilised the forest guards as a military unit and four decrees, the last of which appeared on 29 August 1870, placed them at the disposal of the Minister of War. Most of them were based in Paris, where they formed a regiment of forest guards of two battalions.

Some units stayed in the provinces as the Germans troops invaded where they almost all took shelter in those fortresses put under siege. A total of 11 forest companies were organised in the provinces. One of them was locked up in Metz and five others were occupied in the defence of fortresses. This left only five companies of forest guards employed in the provincial armies. Among the latter, only one was specially recruited: the company of volunteer forest guides, formed in Toulouse on 1 December, with men from the departments of Ariège and Haute-Garonne. This company included, as officers, a sub-inspector and six general guards. It joined, on 18 December, in Bourges, the Army of the Loire and was assigned to the 15th Corps. Three other companies, formed with the forest guards of the departments of the 8th Military Division, were added to a battalion of volunteers – the scouts of the Lyon National Guard – and there formed the legion of scouts of the 8th Division, under the orders of a general guard forest ranger. This legion occupied the Côte-d'Or from the beginning of November and was linked during its operations to General Cremer's division. Finally, the *Compagnie des Guides Forestiers des Ardennes* operated in its own department. Many forest guards enlisted either in the mobilised national guard, or in the volunteer corps, where they served as instructors.

The company of forest guards of Jura and Moselle, formed on 10 August, were deployed to defend Thionville and a detachment was sent to Longwy; the company of forest guards of Yonne, composed of three officers and 66 men, remained in Auxerre; the three companies of forest guards of Haute-Marne (Langres, Chaumont and Vassy) were assigned to the defence of Langres. These three companies were amalgamated on 25 December. Good use was made of the foresters during the siege of Paris, using their knowledge of the country they were able to carry messages to and from the beleaguered city without being detected.

When first raised they were clothed completely in green: *habit*, vest, and trousers with white metal buttons. As with the French Army generally, in 1852 the tailcoat was replaced by a tunic described as being 'dragoon green' in colour and with similar collar, cuffs and shoulder straps. The pointed cuffs had yellow piping and a yellow tab was fixed to the front of the collar. It was closed by a single row of nine white metal buttons. Blue-grey trousers were piped green. In full dress a green cloth-covered shako, with yellow lace round the top and yellow piping on each side, black leather top and peak and a double green pompon was worn. On the front was a painted metal tricolour cockade, a large brass imperial eagle standing on a plaque bearing the legend 'FORÊTS'. In the field the forester guards wore a jockey-style cap, in green with a black leather peak and a yellow hunting horn badge. Black belts completed the ensemble.

Officers had a similar uniform with silver piping on the pointed cuffs, silver-edged shoulder straps and a silver decoration on either side of the collar. They wore grey gloves and had a kepi in green with silver piping. Rank was shown by silver lace round the cuffs and on the lower band of the kepi.

Those men who had been brought into Paris and had to endure the siege were dressed in a green double-breasted tunic with two rows of five white metal buttons and a yellow hunting horn badge on the front of the collar. They had blue-grey trousers piped yellow as well as a green kepi with yellow piping and a yellow hunting horn badge on the front.

Garibaldi's volunteers

At the beginning of the war Garibaldi announced his support for the Prussians and hoped they would quickly chastise Napoleon (whom he detested). However, with the fall of the empire he changed his mind and urged his followers to save the new French Republic. He turned up in Marseilles and offered his services to the French authorities, much to their embarrassment. Eventually they gave him a command in the east of France protecting the city of Lyon from the unlikely threat of any German advance in that direction. Volunteers from all over Europe rallied to his name and the collected troops were given the title the 'Army of the Vosges'. All the available volunteers were grouped together, every unit of different size, although they called themselves 'companies', 'battalions', 'legions', or other outlandish names. Some chose to name themselves after their place of origin, some after their nationality, others patriotic slogans.

Each unit was armed and equipped differently, which was a nightmare supply problem for the Chief of Staff, auxiliary General Philippe Toussaint Joseph Bordone. Of course, the non-French volunteers wanted to show their enthusiasm for Garibaldi and wear the famous red shirt, but only a few managed to get them. There were small groups of mounted men acting as scouts and even some small artillery units, including a battery of *Mitrailleuses*. According to a report from General Bordone, the army was divided into four brigades:

Sketches by Emelé, a war artist, of Garibaldini volunteers, December 1870.

1st Brigade, Staff Colonel Stefano Canzio, later General Josef Bossak-Haucke:
Genoa Carbineers
Italian or Marsalla Legion
Spanish Company
Franco–Spanish Company
De Grey Scouts
Egyptian *Chasseurs*
Francs-tireurs of the Midi
Francs-tireurs of Philippeville
Francs-tireurs of the Rhone
Company of Algiers
42nd Regiment of Mobiles of the Aveyron
1st Legion of Mobiles of the Isere
Battery of artillery

2nd Brigade, Colonel Lobbina:
1st Battalion of Equals of Marseille
2nd Battalion of Equals of Marseille
Marseille Guerrillas
French Guerrillas of the East
Garibaldian Skirmishers of the Var
Company of Sailors
Francs-tireurs of the Atlas
Mounted Scouts

3rd Brigade, Menotti Garibaldi:
1st Auxiliary Mobiles of the Alpes-Maritime
2nd Auxiliary Mobiles of the Alpes-Maritime
Battalion of Mobiles of the Lower Alps
Battalion of Mobiles of the Lower Pyrenees
3rd Legion of the Mobiles of the Isere
Italian Volunteer Legion
Legion of *Chasseurs* of the Alps
Battalion of Reunited *Francs-tireurs*
Vaucluse Company
Oran Company
Company of *Francs-tireurs*

4th Brigade, Ricciotti Garibaldi:
2nd Legion of Mobiles of the Isere
Nicolai Battalion
Scout Company of the Allier
Chasseur Company of Savoy and Mont Blanc
Francs-Tireurs of the Aveyron
1st and 2nd Companies of the *Chasseurs* of the Dauphinois
Scouts of the Doubs
Francs-Tireurs of the Cotes-d'Or
Francs-Tireurs of Dole

Francs-Tireurs of the Croix-de-Nice
Francs-Tireurs of Toulouse
Francs-Tireurs of the Vosges
1st Company of the Gers
Chasseurs of the Loire
1st Company of Bigorre and Jonzac
Revenge Company
Company of the Crescent
Company of the Lost Children of the Mountain
Company of Caprera

Two batteries of mountain guns and a platoon of the 7th *Chasseurs à cheval* were attached to the Army of the Vosges.

Garibaldi's volunteers. (Watercolour by Maurice Toussaint)

The uniforms adopted by the volunteers of all nationalities fighting under the command of Garibaldi was to be the famous red shirt, although in many cases this proved not to be possible. The most common garment was a red blouse with a fly front closed by three buttons which was tucked into the trousers of various shades of grey. Sometimes the blouse would be worn tunic length. Officers would adopt a similarly coloured tunic, single- or double-breasted. Headgear was the most varied part of the uniform, from the basic kepi with red top and green band, alternatively a short round cap, termed an 'American cap' often in waterproof material, to a peaked cap, similar to the Prussian field cap, with a red top and coloured band. Civilian-type hats were popular, black with a narrow brim, or grey felt with a wide brim, often decorated with a feather. The waist sash was almost universal, but usually of blue wool to distinguish it from the red blouse. Black shoes or whatever they could get hold of were worn by the men, with officers favouring calf- or even knee-length boots. In keeping with Garibaldi's philosophy, equipment was usually at a minimum, say a black waistbelt and pouch. Most volunteers got hold of a Chassepot rifle and bayonet, while a few lucky individuals were issued with Winchester repeaters.

Irish Volunteers

There was an outburst of sympathy for the French cause in Ireland and a volunteer ambulance was organised to assist the French medical services. The ambulance consisted of 31 surgeons, 250 men, five wagons, and tents and bedding which paraded for the first time at the Rotunda Gardens in Dublin on 8 October 1870 under the command of Dr Charles P Baxter. It then sailed to France, arriving on 11 October and serving until February 1871. The corps supported the new Republican Armies of the North and the Loire. The only Irish casualty was a wagon-driver, William Hopkins, who died of smallpox in November. Upon arrival in France, it was apparent that there were too many 'helpers' to be of use to the medical team and some of the Irish volunteers decided that they wanted to fight. They formed *La Compagnie Irlandaise* (The Irish Company) of the 2nd Foreign Infantry Regiment, led by Irishman Martin Waters Kirwan. The company initially paraded in the middle of October at Caen with three officers, a surgeon and 93 NCOs and men to which was added three French sergeants to help with training. They were one of the last French units in action and were engaged in combat as the rear guard of the last battalion of the French Army crossing over into Switzerland The uniform of the 2nd Regiment was the standard French infantry dress, with a red star on the kepi in place of the regimental number and green fringed epaulettes with red crescents.

Postal Service

At the end of September, the Ministry of Finance took the necessary measures to provide the 15th Corps, then in training at Bourges, with a military treasury and post office. A number of postal officials had been called upon to assist in this service. Several others, moreover, endeavoured to establish communications either with the places under siege, or with the invaded departments. From15 October 1870, the military telegraphy service was run by the officials and agents of the telegraph administration. Under these conditions, a decree of 1 November 1870 decided that 'the personnel of the administration of telegraphs and posts, seconded to the armies, or assigned to the defence service of a place or a territory in a state of siege, or fulfilling a war mission, would be considered and treated as part of the army'.

A little later, in order to activate the postal service, it seemed rational to the Government of National Defence to separate the post office from the military treasury and closely link the postal service to the armed forces to the general service of the territory. A decree of 27 November regularised this new state of affairs and subordinated to the Director General of Telegraphs and Posts the postal agents serving with the troops in the field, charging them with ensuring the transport and handling of correspondence to the armies.

A series of decrees fixed the composition of the personnel of the postal service attached to the various army corps; it included, under the direction of a senior officer, a number of clerks, couriers and guards. To simplify the accounting and facilitate operations, the heads of service in each army corps, either a director or controller, were responsible for directly providing for all expenses.

New Weapons

The French Army had started the war with probably the best European designed rifle, referred to as the 'Chassepot' after its designer. Compared to the Prussian Dreyse, it had a smaller calibre, flatter trajectory, and longer range. The small size of the cartridge meant that the individual soldier could carry more ammunition than his German counterpart. However, it still had features that meant it was already becoming outdated. The cartridge was made up of a bullet, powder and ignition held in a paper and linen cover which was consumed by the force of the explosion. An English war correspondent noted that:

> Whilst looking at these things with considerable interest (view over Metz), the sharp report of the chassepot, followed by the ping of a bullet to the left, made me turn my glass in that direction, and I saw a small patrol of the King's Hussars cantering away towards Malmaison (farm, near Metz) with one empty saddle. I found out afterwards that it was unfortunately the officer commanding the patrol, who had ventured somewhat too near the French works, and had been shot through the head. Poor fellow! He was an only son, and the head of an old family. In order to illustrate the fearful range of a chassepot bullet, I may say that Captain von Loe, the officer in question, dropped from his saddle, the men thinking he had swooned, as they none of them heard any report, so far off was the man who fired. I also am intimately acquainted with an officer who was wounded three times consecutively and had never seen a French soldier.[7]

The newly designed Bavarian rifle, designated the Werder, commonly called the 'Lightning' rifle, because of its high rate of fire, used a metallic cartridge with the case being ejected after firing during reloading. A trained soldier could fire up to 20 aimed shots in a minute. Sadly, for the Bavarians, they were only just being issued with relatively few in the hands of the troops. The remainder had to make do with possibly the worst rifle of the war: the Podewils, a muzzle-loader converted to breach-loader.

The French government issued orders to factories throughout France not under German occupation to try and replace the huge number of Chassepots lost, destroyed or captured in the first three months of the war. Not only in France, but factories in England and Italy also received contracts to manufacture Chassepots. Some factories and workshops lying in the path of the German advance were dismantled and re-erected in safe areas, such as Bordeaux, or even as far south as Bayonne near the Spanish border.

The excellent *Fusil d'infanterie Modele 1866* (the official designation of the Chassepot rifle) equipped the 340,000 men of the French field armies in July 1870, with a further 680,000 held in the regimental depots and arsenals. The sabre bayonets with which they were issued were made in factories in Alsace (including the famous Klingenthal steel works, which had been making blades for the French Army since the time of Louis XV) and were also subcontracted to steel works in Birmingham (Webley), Brecia in Italy, Liege in Belgium and also by Y. Funke & Coy. in Prussia. Huge stocks of older weapons were held in government armouries, and they were modernised by transforming the loading system from muzzle to breech *a la tabatière* (the opening at the breech looked like a contemporary snuff box lid). Over 190,000

7 Sir Randal H. Roberts, *Modern War, or the Campaigns of the First Prussian Army, 1870–71* (London: Chapman & Hall, 1871).

such transformations were carried out by gun factories at St Etienne. Smaller numbers were converted to breech-loading by fitting a bolt action in factories all over France, as the factories in Alsace were occupied by the Germans. Buyre produced 21,000 conversions at Lyon, and Hurtu & Hautin, delivered 10,000 rifles and carbines with bayonets. Mouraille at Toulon and Perre at Avignon were also given contracts. All these weapons used the 18 mm cartridge. Rivolier produced rifles with the breech using the Remington 'Rolling Block' system. A native design was the carbine-revolver of Perrin, using a six-shot cylinder and having a Chassepot-type bayonet which fitted on to the barrel by means of a tubular sleeve.

Many pistols, single-shot muzzle-loaders, were still in service, with models for cavalry, staff officers and infantry officers. Various models of revolver were also available, with the official weapon being the Model 1858, a six-shooter with a metal cartridge in 11 mm made by Lefaucheux. Galand and Perrin also produced revolvers using a 12 mm cartridge (but not interchangeable). The Le Mat revolver had a nine-shot cylinder firing 9 mm rounds and a separate barrel firing a single 11 mm bullet. Officers were given an allowance to buy a pistol of their choice.

The Montigny *Mitrailleuse* was an early type of crank-operated machine-gun (technically a volley gun, as all chambers were fired consecutively, whence the breech had to be reloaded with fresh ammunition after each discharge) developed by the Belgian gun works of Joseph Montigny between 1859 and 1870. Some 215 were manufactured for the French Army before the Franco–Prussian War of 1870–1871. Unfortunately, the tactics for using such a weapon had not been sufficiently thought through. To most French soldiers it looked like a piece of artillery, therefore that was how it was used, in batteries and at its extreme range.

Imported Weapons

United States

Most prominent among the weapons from the United States were the Model 1855 Springfield rifled muskets and various Spencer repeating rifles and carbines – the latter chambered for the .56–56, .56–52 and .56–50 Spencer rimfire cartridges.

At the end of the Civil War, the American government tested various rifles to find a suitable breech-loading, metallic cartridge rifle for the Army. Trials were held with dozens of different models; large numbers of some of them were manufactured for field testing though never adopted.

American gun makers were producing breech-loading rifles for domestic and overseas sales and having expanded their production facilities during the Civil War, were capable of turning out large numbers of weapons. Prominent among these were the Remington of New York's rolling block action rifle, which by 1870 had already been adopted by several armies around the world.

Although several countries had ordered the Remington, French government agents came with pockets full of cash and the company had no qualms about diverting production to a customer who could pay there and then. The Egyptian Army had ordered 100,000 examples and the French took them all, plus a further 50,000 as they rolled off the production lines. This excellent breech-loader was made in 11.2 mm calibre and fired the .44-inch Remington Egyptian cartridge with a lead bullet in a brass case. A further 15,000 rifles destined for the Greek Army also ended up in France, which fortunately were chambered for the same cartridge. Each weapon cost the French treasury 100 francs (approximately £65 today).

A proposal to equip the US Navy with a Remington rifle, built at the Springfield Arsenal in Massachusetts, was rejected by naval inspectors, even though production was well under way. Nearly 17,000 were immediately snapped up and given the designation 'Remington Marine 1870'. It was supplied with a sabre bayonet and fired a Springfield .50-inch calibre bullet.

A further Remington obtained by the French was the model made for the Spanish Army, similar in construction to the Egyptian model, but chambered for a .433-inch bullet. About 3,700 were delivered. The Remington carbine, although 21,000 were delivered, was little used because of its limited range of about 150 metres.

A number of muzzle-loaders were obtained, including the Harpers Ferry Model 1855 firing a .58 calibre bullet and equipped with a sabre bayonet. Over a third of a million Springfield percussion rifles of the same calibre were delivered: models of 1861 and 1863 with spike bayonets. Compared to the Chassepot they had limited range, being sited up to 500 yards. Many muzzle-loaders were converted to breech-loaders firing a variety of .58-inch cartridges. Some were converted by Remington – over 19,000 Berdan system conversions at Springfield Arsenal – and over 63,000 by Colt. A further 25,000 weapons were converted by the Allin system, but with a smaller calibre of .50-inch.

As well as rifles, the Americans also sold the French government over 90,000 carbines for use by cavalry and artillery, and ultimately the volunteers. The Spencer Repeating Rifle Company produced a seven-shot rifle in two models: the 'Army' with a spike bayonet, and a 'Navy' with a sword bayonet. Over 8,500 of these were delivered to France. In far greater numbers was the Spencer carbine, also with a seven-shot charger, 46,000 being supplied. In 1860 Benjamin Tyler Henry developed a rifle with a tubular magazine under the barrel which went into production as the '1866 Winchester' also in two versions: a rifle holding 13 rounds and having a spike bayonet, and a carbine holding 15 rounds. They arrived late during the war and the only record of their use was by a unit of Garibaldi's Army of the Vosges at Dijon in January 1871. A battalion of the Prussian 61st Regiment was decimated during the fighting, all the colour party was shot down, and the Garibaldians recovered the battalion's flag from the battlefield the following day. Both versions fired the Henry .44-inch rimfire cartridge, a lead bullet atop a brass case. A total of 3,000 of each model was delivered. Other carbines arrived at various times through the ports of Brest, Bordeaux, Le Havre and Cherbourg. The Ball carbine had been ordered by the US government in 1864, but not delivered until May 1865, after the war was over. Some 1,000 were in store when a French agent bought them up. The carbine held a charger with seven rounds of .56-inch calibre.

Small numbers of American-made carbines arrived in France during the latter part of 1870 and early 1871, including 2,500 Gallagher from Richardson and Overman of Philadelphia, 1,600 Joslyns, and 1,000 Palmer carbines from E.G. Lamson and Co. of Vermont – all unfortunately using ammunition of different calibres.

Factories in the US manufactured vast quantities of revolvers, which, when shipped over to France equipped mounted troops and found their way into the arsenals of many of the *Garde Mobile* and volunteer units. Over 85,000 such weapons from Remington New Model 1863, Colt New Model Army 1860, Colt Navy 1851, and Starr Army 1858 adorned the belts of infantry and cavalry alike, as evidenced by contemporary photographs. The Smith & Wesson Number 2 was small-calibre revolver firing a .32-inch (8 mm) bullet. Several Remington Navy pistols, Model 1865 and Model 1867, were obtained, these were single-shot, breech-loaders.

An unknown number of Gatling guns arrived in cases in ports on the Atlantic coast and were used by the new French armies raised in the west, while others were manufactured within Paris during the siege. Their tactical use was as yet untried, and they, like the *Mitrailleuses* of the imperial army, were more of a morale booster for the French than useful for their destructive power.

Great Britain

Factories in England supplied several thousand rifles to the French government, including 50,000 Enfield rifles of .577-inch calibre with a range of 990 metres and 10,000 old percussion guns converted *a la tabatière* by the Snider system. These weapons went mainly to the French Army of the North, the troops in Normandy and the Army of Brittany. Also, over 20,000 Model 1866 Chassepot rifles were made in the UK. The US Peabody rifle was made in British factories, as were some of Colt revolvers.

Chassepot rifles were made in Belgium and Austria as well as France. French agents in Italy obtained over 4,000 Model 1822 French muskets converted to breech-loaders using the Carcano bolt action system (a native design similar to the actions of the Dreyse and Chassepot).

Codes and Ciphers

Sending messages in code has a long history; when only a few people were literate a simple code, as used by Julius Caesar, where one letter was replaced by another, was sufficient. This cipher using two copies of the alphabet laid below one another with one set moved a specified number of spaces by a prearranged plan was all that was needed. However, once the idea caught on, this code was relatively simple to break. The need for more sophisticated ciphers developed and with the increasing use of diplomacy at government level by the mid-1600s the Frenchman Antoine Rossignol had developed an almost uncrackable system of codes. Instead of changing letters it was based on the spoken word with codes for syllables. Rossignol was a mathematician and ran France's early intelligence service, keeping a check on both political enemies of the king and criminal suspects. This was fine for diplomatic correspondence where time was not of the essence, but to send military instructions in code which could not be read quickly could lead to disaster. Rossignol's code, 'The Great Cipher', was maintained by members of his family for nearly 200 years until the last of the family died in 1811 and it fell out of use. (There apparently are still many documents in the French archives that have never been deciphered.)

The cipher used by the French in 1870 was loosely based on Rossignol's work, but in a simplified form. It was ideal for diplomatic exchanges, but the code had few useful military terms in its vocabulary – 'not fit for purpose' in modern language. Even Bazaine, marching on Metz, complained to the Ministry of War in Paris that the cipher was useless as it did not contain any of the usual technical terms used in war.

For all their forward-looking military innovations, the Prussians still used a variant of Julius Caesar's letter transposition, the Gronsfeld cipher. It was invented by a Belgian diplomat in the 1740s, again for his diplomatic correspondence, but with the letter shift indicated by a number key. Some messages from the German Army's headquarters did get intercepted by the French intelligence service who had no difficulty reading them, but as events moved quickly with the German's advance and the French retreats this proved of little benefit.

Both sides ciphers relied on a code book and officers trained to use it. In one instance a French staff officer was cut off from his commanding officer's headquarters for two days taking his code book with him (staff officers had been ordered never to let it out of their sight), by the time the officer was able to decode the messages in the headquarters 'in tray', it was, of course, too late to act upon them.

Camps of Instruction

The leaders of the Army of the Second Empire, although well trained in fighting the Arabs across the deserts of Algeria and adequate when faced with native troops in Africa and Asia, realised that some means should be found to handle large bodies of men in Europe. The answer had been the Camp of Instruction at Mourmelon, a military camp of 10,000 hectares, 38 square miles of open country, 22 kilometres (14 miles) north of the city of Chalons in the Champagne region, east of Paris. It was inaugurated on 30 August 1857.

The initial purpose was simply practising military manoeuvres with a large body of men, of corps strength, over 20,000. Unfortunately, it quickly turned into a showcase for Napoleon's army, more of a theatrical display, very much to impress his guests, French politicians and visiting dignitaries from all over Europe and where Frenchmen, particularly Parisians, could watch and be impressed by the army and watch parades. The camp had a few brick buildings, set in an open windswept plain. However, each year at the time for manoeuvres, the camp was transformed into a city of tents and wooden chalets.

The new Republican government took to this idea (in fact an old idea used by Louis XV in the 1750s to train men during the wars against Frederick the Great) and decided that while companies of mobiles, even battalions, could be trained in town squares and fields adjoining villages, really large formations needed purpose-built Camps of Instruction.

An outpost of Garde Mobiles between forts Bicetre and Ivry during the defence of Paris, October 1870. (*Illustrated London News*)

The Army of Brittany was presented with just such a camp about 25 kilometres northwest of Le Man at the village of Conlie. However, it turned out to be an example of how not to do it. The Conlie camp was just one of 11 created across the country in areas far from the front line. (As the Germans advanced against the French 2nd Army of the Loire after the fighting around Le Mans it suddenly became part of the front line.) Another camp was set up by the port of Cherbourg, capable of holding 25,000 men drawn from all over Normandy, but it was barely used.

Count Emile de Kératry, like Gambetta, escaped from Paris by balloon. He was an opposition member of the French parliament, and on 22 October was appointed general of the new Army of Brittany, yet to be formed. Kératry was promised several million francs and arms (he insisted on Chassepots) and equipment and on 25 October ordered an engineer called Armand Rousseau to begin work on a large camp. In five weeks, the camp was laid out capable of holding 50,000 men. A call was sent out all over Brittany for volunteers, who very soon began to arrive. But what did they find? The camp had been built across a level plateau of farmland which had just been ploughed ready for planting and then it had rained heavily, turning the ground into a huge quagmire. It quickly gained the name '*Kerfank*' – a Breton word meaning 'City of Mud'.

The administration was quickly overwhelmed, though some uniforms and equipment arrived and even a few weapons, but hardly any Chassepots. The men had tents to shelter from the weather, but no way of combatting the mud which was by now up to their knees. In such conditions disease soon appeared, including cases of smallpox. Supplies continued to arrive, but experienced NCOs and officers were lacking, so little actual military training was done. An inventory of arms was made on 23 November when the strength of the Army of Brittany stood at 24,000 men. There were just 2,000 Chassepots; but 5,000 Spencer carbines without bayonets; 2,000 Egyptian model Remingtons; 1,800 Sniders; 9,000 various muzzle-loaders and 500 revolvers. There were also 20 old pieces of artillery to defend the camp

French engineers. (Watercolour by Maurice Toussaint)

and some 12- and 4-pounders to form several field batteries. There were even seven Gatling guns, recently delivered from the United States. By 13 December the number of officers and men at the camp stood at 49,000, with five batteries of artillery and a squadron of cuirassiers (six officers and 133 troopers from the 3rd Regiment).

After the battle of Le Mans the Germans captured the Conlie camp and found it partially destroyed but still containing large amounts of stores and equipment, which they happily took over for their own use.

Other camps were situated at St Omer (for training the Army of the North), La Rochelle, Pas-des-Lanciers, Nevers, Bordeaux, Clermont-Ferrand, Toulouse, Montpellier, and Lyon. Over eight million francs were spent by the government on the construction and supply of the camps, but by late November, early December any training was largely ineffective and too late to make a decisive contribution to the war.

The Effects of the War on France

After the fall of the empire and the proclamation of the Republic, the new government, dominated by Gambetta, bent its will on raising, arming and equipping vast numbers of men. These men were, by and large, drawn from the peasants who inhabited the small villages and hamlets and farms of the enormous countryside of France. They were somewhat inured to doing as they were commanded, mostly as they had little education and felt honour bound to obey their 'betters' as they saw them. These were men who had some, often rudimentary education, be they local or national politicians, government officials of all classes or men who issued sermons to them from the pulpit on Sundays. They probably had little grasp of what it was they were fighting for, only they knew what they were against, albeit they had never clapped eyes on a 'German' of any description before. The middle classes and the more politically inclined citizens of the large cities were more aware of what was involved and those with an education quickly filled the positions of company officers. If they were lucky, they learnt the rudiments of their new trade before they were killed, wounded, sickened or captured. The peasant soldiers marched backwards and forwards, often cold, wet, hungry and dispirited, as they were bid. Occasionally they got to fire their weapons, hopefully pointing in the right direction.

But those not in uniform also had to pay for the war. They still owed their taxes to the government, but as armies came and went across the country, they were expected to feed and house them. Soldiers ate up the peasant's food, killed their chickens and drove off their cattle and horses. It mattered little to a farmer if the soldier wore red trousers and a kepi on his head or a blue tunic and a leather helmet with a brass spike. French soldiers carried camp equipment and were expected to live in the open; German soldiers were billeted in towns, villages, farms, sheds and barns and as all soldiers do, cooked their food over fires that were fed with anything combustible, fences, furniture included. The Germans also requisitioned anything the country could supply – beer in Alsace, sparkling wine in Champagne and tobacco everywhere. Bread and boots were other constant items on the list of goods to be supplied.

Where requisitions were made it was the responsibility of the mayor and local authorities to fulfil it. In the town of Dieppe there were a number of factories processing tobacco (a government monopoly) and the Germans demanded a quantity for the use of the 8th Corps. The mayor procrastinated, pleading that although the raw tobacco was in the stores there was not the time to manufacture it for use of the troops. The German commander therefore demanded the town pay a fine of 120,000 francs by the next morning. (A loaf of bread cost between 50 centimes and one franc.) The penalty for not paying would be the destruction of the town and the imprisonment of the mayor and his council in a camp in Germany. The mayor and town council paid the fine. Town councils exercised considerable power among the local populace and with sections of the army, particularly the *Gardes Mobiles*, who were, after all, private citizens who had only just put on unforms. During the fighting around Orleans some *Mobiles* were informed of the presence of Prussian troops in the nearby town of Beaugency and advanced to try to eject them. The council quickly contacted the *Mobiles* and asked them not to come any closer as they did not want to see fighting which would damage the town. The *Mobiles* obliged and took a circuitous route to avoid the town.

A number of middle-class citizens decided not to heed Gambetta's call and left the country, taking up residence in Belgium or England. The father of the 'Impressionist' style of painting, Camile Pissarro, left Paris and brought his family to Norwood, then a small village on the edge of London. With his friend, Claude Monet, he paid visits to the National Gallery in London and they were impressed by the style and techniques of John Constable and William Turner. The first 'Impressionist Exhibition' was held in Paris in 1874.

Art, Artists, Musicians and Writers

Ernest Meissonier (1815–1891)

A history and battle painter, Meissonier had experience as a soldier during the Revolution of 1848 in Paris as a captain in the National Guard. During the Second Empire his work was admired by Napoleon, and Meissonier was given a government commission to paint scenes from the Franco–Austrian War of 1859 as a member of the imperial staff. In 1870 he was again on the staff and was given the colonelcy of a provisional infantry regiment during the siege of Paris.

Edouard Detaille (1848–1912)

Detaille was a pupil of Meissonier and followed his style with his great attention to the finer details of his works. In 1870 he enlisted in the 8th Battalion of *Gardes Mobiles* and witnessed the war at first hand. He was particularly careful to depict accurately uniforms and scenes of military life. He became the French official painter of the war. Detaille went on to produce the book called *L'Armee Francaise* in 1885 and in 1912 designed a series of army uniforms, which, however, were not adopted, but did influence the later '*horizon bleu*' uniforms introduced in 1915.

French Fusilier Marines. (Drawing by Edouard Detaille)

Paul Grolleron (1848–1901)

Grolleron focused on historical and military subjects, and particularly scenes of the War of 1870, which were appreciated by both the public and the academic juries. He won a third-class medal at the Salon of 1886, a bronze medal at the *Exposition Universelle* of 1889, and a second-class medal '*hors concours*' at the Salon of 1894.

Lionel Royer (1852–1926)

Royer was born in Château-du-Loir in Sarthe on 25 December 1852. He volunteered before his 18th birthday for the army and took part in the Battle of Loigny-Poupry on 2 December 1870. In memory of his participation in the battle of Loigny, he donated two paintings to the rebuilt church of this village, the first representing the mass attended by the volunteers before leaving for the battle and the second depicting the agony of the severely wounded General de Sonis who lay on the battlefield during the bitterly cold night with a wound that eventually led to the amputation of his leg.

Maurice Orange (1867–1916)

Orange's youth was spent with his family and was influenced by the War. He showed an early talent for drawing and his first tutors gained him a scholarship to the *École des Beaux-Arts* in 1885, where he studied under Jean-Léon Gérôme and François Flameng. He was mainly inspired by historical subjects, especially the Napoleonic era, though he also produced portraits, landscapes, townscapes and sketches, often adding drawings to his letters. He painted 'heroic' battle scenes and accurate depictions of troops and their dress and equipment.

Édouard Castres (1838–1902)

Castres studied fine arts in Geneva before enrolling in the *École des Beaux-Arts* in Paris. He took part in the War of 1870–1871 as a Red Cross volunteer accompanying General Bourbaki's Eastern Army throughout the last phase of the war. With collaborators he executed, in 1881, a large-scale panorama showing the withdrawal of Bourbaki's army into Switzerland and its internment. This panorama is displayed in a rotunda in Lucerne. The circular Bourbaki Panorama depicts the internment of the French *Armée de l'Est* in neutral Switzerland at the end of the war. The army, led by General Charles-Denis Bourbaki, had been defeated in the field while attempting to raise the siege of Belfort and retreated to Switzerland. The Swiss admitted the French soldiers, and local villagers and the Swiss Red Cross provided aid.

To prepare for the commission Castres spent the winter of 1876–1877 at Verrières, sketching and painting the landscape to help him to reproduce it more accurately on the panorama. Castres worked on the panorama for five months with a team of ten painters who went largely uncredited. He wanted to create a sense of atmosphere and so painted the panorama as if the viewer was within the scene, not looking down upon it from higher ground. The sense of atmosphere and depth was heightened by the inclusion of three-dimensional objects in the foreground, in front of the painting, when it was exhibited. These objects included figures, military equipment and even a railway carriage.

The painting focuses on the meeting of French General Justin Clinchant (to whom Bourbaki had handed command of the *Armée de l'Est*) and the Swiss General Hans Herzog in front of the Hôtel Fédéral. The rest of the scene shows a line of weary and wounded French soldiers trekking through a snow-covered valley to pile their arms under the supervision of the Swiss Bernese Battalion. Some of the Frenchmen are being assisted by local residents and members of the Red Cross. Rail lines and straight roads provide axes of perspective. The circumference of the finished work, painted in oils on canvas, is 115 metres (377 feet). The panorama is unusual in depicting the tragic consequences of war, rather than the usual celebration of victory. It also acts as a reminder of Swiss neutrality and hospitality.

Frédéric Bazille (1841–1870)

Bazille's close circle included Claude Monet, Alfred Sisley and Édouard Manet. Bazille joined a zouave regiment in August 1870, a month after the outbreak of the war. On 28 November he was with his unit serving as an enlisted man in the 3rd Auxiliary Regiment of Zouaves at the Battle of Beaune-la-Rolande when, his officer having been injured, he took command and led an assault on the German position. He was hit twice in the failed attack and died on the battlefield at the age of 28. His father travelled to the battlefield a few days later to take his body back for burial at Montpellier.

Pierre-Auguste Renoir (1841–1919)

During the Commune some Communards found Renoir painting on the banks of the River Seine, thought he was a spy and were about to throw him into the river when one of the most bloodthirsty leaders of the Commune, Raoul Rigault, recognised Renoir as the man who had protected him on an earlier occasion. Rigault intervened and vouched for him. By this slender thread, Renoir was saved to go on to become one of the giants of Impressionist painting.

Claude Monet (1840–1926)

On the outbreak of the war Monet and his friend Pissarro fled to England. While there he studied the work of Constable and Turner and met the art dealer Durand-Ruel, who was to become one of the great champions of the Impressionists.

Camille Pissarro (1830–1903)

At the beginning of the war the painter Pissarro moved his family to Norwood, then a village on the southern edge of London. During his stay Pissarro painted scenes at Sydenham and Norwood at a time when they were semi-rural and had only just been connected to London by railway. Twelve oil paintings date from his stay including 'The Avenue, Sydenham' (now in the London National Gallery), 'Norwood Under the Snow' and 'Lordship Lane Station'. He had produced some 1,500 paintings over the preceding 20 years – works which gave evidence of the birth of Impressionism. Tragically, when he returned to France after the Commune, Pissarro discovered that out of this huge body of work, only 40 paintings had survived. The rest had been damaged or destroyed by the soldiers, who used them, among other things, as doormats or to wipe their boots.

Émile Zola (1840–1902)

Zola's father was an Italian engineer with some Greek ancestry born in Venice in 1795 and engineered the Zola Dam in Aix-en-Provence. Zola's mother was French. The family moved to Aix-en-Provence in the southeast when Émile was three years old. Four years later, in 1847, his father died, leaving his mother a meagre pension. In 1858, the Zolas moved to Paris, where Émile's childhood friend Paul Cézanne soon joined him. Zola started to write in the romantic style. His widowed mother had planned a law career for Émile, but he failed his baccalaureate examination twice. Before his breakthrough as a writer, Zola worked for minimal pay as a clerk in a shipping firm and then in the sales department for the publisher Hachette. He also wrote literary and art reviews for newspapers. As a political journalist, Zola did not hide his dislike of Napoleon III.

Zola's novel *La Débâcle* (published in English as *The Downfall*) was published in 1892 and was the penultimate in *Les Rougon-Macquart* series. The story is set against the background of the political and military tumults that ended the reign of Napoléon III and the Second Empire in 1870, particularly the war, the Battle of Sedan and the Paris Commune. The novel is by far the longest of the Rougon-Macquart series. Its main character is Jean Macquart, a farmer who after having lost his wife and land (in the novel *La Terre*), has joined the army for the campaign of 1870. The main theme is the brutality of war for the common soldier and the civilian population, hit by the death of family and friends and by economic hardship.

Plate 1 Grand Duke Frederick I of Baden at the proclamation of William of Prussia as German emperor.

Plate 2 Prussia, Garrison company, old equipment, single ammunition pouch and short marching boots.

Plate 3 Bavarian infantryman, winter dress, blanket worn 'poncho' style over the greatcoat, locally made sabots stuffed with straw to fit.

Plate 4 Württemberg infantry, 3rd Regiment. Field dress.

Plate 5 Officer of Prussian Landwehr infantry, large case for field glasses.

Plate 6 Prussia, mounted Field Gendarmerie, the army police force in the rear of the front and in the occupied territories.

Plate 7 Prussia, hospital clothing jacket issued to convalescents.

Plate 8 Switzerland, Grenadier company.

Plate 9 Colonel Charles Pynder Beauchamp Walker, uniform of the British Staff Corps, he has taken the undress field cap in place of the plumed cocked hat.

Plate 10 Belgian Carabineer, in the field he would wear the greatcoat and leave the feather plume off.

Plate 11 France, naval Captain Jaurès as a general of division, later he was general of the 21st Corps, after the war he reverted to the navy with the rank of Rear-Admiral.

Plate 12 Volunteer of the West, 2nd Battalion with dark grey cloth uniform.

Plate 13 France, Company of Forest Officials.

Plate 14 France, National Guard drummer, full dress.

Plate 15 Cyprien-Pierre Urbain-Aime, sergeant of the Volunteers of Frouard.

Plate 16 Volunteer, 'Chasseur du Havre'.

Plate 17 Breton Volunteer.

Plate 18 Volunteer of the Aisne, well equipped with two front pouches and chassepot rifle.

Plate 19 Guard Mobile, 3rd company 116th Battalion, armed with a US Remington rifle.

Plate 20 Field Gendarme, Army of the Loire. Police, Judge, jury and, if necessary, executioner!

Henri René Albert Guy de Maupassant (1850–1893)
The war broke out soon after Maupassant's graduation from college in 1870, whereupon he enlisted as a volunteer. He was a master of the short story form, as well as a representative of the Naturalist School, which depicted human lives, destinies and social forces in disillusioned and often pessimistic terms. A protégé of Gustave Flaubert, his stories are characterised by their economy of style. Many are set during the War of 1870–1871 and describe the futility of war and the innocent civilians who, caught up in events beyond their control, are permanently changed by their experiences. Maupassant wrote 300 short stories, six novels, three travel books and one volume of verse.

Gabriel Fauré (1845–1924)
Fauré was 'the master par excellence of French music, the perfect mirror of our musical genius'. So wrote one of his reviewers. His famous 'Requiem' was begun in 1887 and revised and expanded over the years until its final version appeared in 1901. On the outbreak of the war in 1870 he volunteered for military service. He took part in the defence of Paris and saw action at Le Bourget, Champigny and Créteil. Fauré was awarded the *Croix de Guerre.*

Naval Operations

On 4 October 1870, the Minister of the Navy, Admiral Léon Martin Fourichon, sent a telegram to Vice-Admiral Gueydon, commander of part of the North Sea fleet, to patrol the North Sea to prevent German ships leaving Scottish ports to harbours under German control. Their task was made difficult as France respected neutral shipping, provided it was not carrying materials for use in the war. The blockade of the German coast being all but lifted due to lack of ships and coal, those on patrol who remained maintained more of a surveillance role. The French reported that the English were benefiting from the war and that the number of steamers flying the English flag entering and leaving German ports was considerable. Even steaming at their slowest speeds, the French ships were burning prodigious amounts of coal and finding it difficult to resupply. The frigate '*Invincible*' had to put into a harbour near Deal on the Kent coast in order to find coal. In addition, prolonged steaming was proving to have a bad effect on engines and boilers. The minister considered recalling five frigates and three fast dispatch boats and take them out of service. When told to conserve fuel, the admiral replied that his ships relied on sail and only use their engines to stop them drifting. He further explained that while his ships maintained their stations during the day, at night they tended to spread out, which gave the Germans the opportunity to slip past.

The French fleet had the further responsibility of protecting the merchant marine against any possible interreference from German commerce raiders. Although these were few in number, they still presented a threat. The flow of arms and ammunition purchased in America and Britain was vital to the continued resistance of the French Army.

A third task was to observe the Prussian naval stations of Kiel and Wilhelmshaven and report any movements of the enemy fleet and whether it took the opportunity to strike at the French warships. German ships, or neutrals carrying contraband, were ready to cross the North Sea if the French were not careful. The journey from Scotland to the German coast, or through the Skagerrak into the Baltic Sea, was a relatively short trip for a merchantman and large numbers of German trading ships were sheltering in Swedish harbours. The French Navy was aided by French consuls in neutral ports reporting ships and ship movements. One consul based in Edinburgh and Leith reported that ships were preparing to leave Scotland and make for Hamburg, evading the patrols of at least three French warships, who had to return to Dunkirk to replenish their supplies of coal.

In waters far from Europe, the French corvette the *Dupleix* found the smaller Prussian corvette SMS *Hertha* in the harbour at Nagasaki and blockaded her there for the rest of the war.

A view of the French fleet of 1870.

French gunboat on the Seine.

Seaman of the Prussian navy. (Drawing by Richard Knötel)

Prussian navy officer. (Drawing by Richard Knötel)

Prussian marine. (Drawing by Richard Knötel)

It is interesting to follow the action of the only real battle between ships of the contending navies, as it shows the difficulties of sea warfare and tactics in use in 1870. In early November the Prussian gunboat SMS *Meteor* was found at Havana by the French fast dispatch boat the *Bouvet*. The two ships were of roughly equal power and in a display of almost medieval bravado the French commander, Alexandre Franquet, issued a challenge to the Prussian commander, Lieutenant Edward von Knorr, to engage in combat, which was accepted. The *Bouvet* left the harbour on 8 November and waited for the *Meteor* to come out. The following day the *Meteor*, escorted by two Spanish warships (to ensure Spanish neutrality, Cuba was then a Spanish colony) steamed towards the *Bouvet*. The conditions at sea were quoted as 'a slight swell', but it was enough to disrupt the aim of both ships. This demonstrates the difficulty of aiming a gun at an erratic target while on a platform that was also moving randomly. For two hours the French and Prussian ships circled each other and exchanged fire without making any hits, until the *Bouvet* increased speed and attempted to ram the Prussian. Lieutenant Knorr realised the danger just in time and turned his ship to present an oblique target. Although it was struck a glancing blow the Prussian ship was not seriously damaged, but the shock collapsed part of the masts and some rigging lines which fell over the side caught in the vessel's propeller. The *Meteor* was now unable to make any headway and the *Bouvet* prepared to repeat the tactic, when a shell from the German gun at last found a target and damaged the French ship's boiler, rendering her unable to move under engine power. The French hoisted sail and made it back to Havana harbour before the crew of the *Meteor* could free their rudder. The two Spanish ships now intervened, bringing the battle to a close. Both sides regarded the honours of battle as equal and both captains received a promotion for

Vice-Admiral Jackmann.

Prince Adalbert of Prussia.

French gunboats on the Loire, captured at Orleans by the Prussians. (*The Graphic*)

their efforts and von Knorr the Iron Cross. The *Meteor* remained in Havana until the end of the war, first to make repairs and second due to French diplomatic pressure on the Spanish government not to complete the works too quickly. Both vessels used steam power to manoeuvre at sea, but, if necessary, they could change to sail – not just to save coal as the French fleet did in the Channel and North Sea, but also as a supplementary power source during an action.

The *Meteor*, weighing 465 tons, as built had a three-masted schooner rig and two boilers powering a marine engine rated at 320 horsepower which could develop a speed of nine knots. It was armed with a 24-pounder gun (15 cm/5.9 inches) and two 12-pounder guns (12 cm/4.7 inches) all rifled breech-loaders. The crew of 71 officers and men also carried plenty of small arms, and during the ramming attempt by the *Bouvet*, a fire fight broke out between them and the crew of the French vessel.

The *Bouvet* was the larger ship at 760 tons, with similar armament – one 16 cm gun and two 12 cm guns – and crew of 85. The poor design of the *Bouvet* led to part of its engine, a steam pipe, being open to the deck and thus unprotected. The single shot from the *Meteor* at close range damaged this pipe, which led to the loss of engine pressure and prevented it from any further powered motion.

Losses on either side were mainly from small arms fire when the two ships were close to each other. The two Prussian sailors who were killed were buried in a cemetery in Havana.

Naval combat between the German *Meteor* and French *Bouvet* off Havana. (Painting by Willy Stower)

View of various vessels from the Prussian navy, from left to right the *Friedrich Karl*, *König Wilhelm* and *Kronprinz*. (Painting by Hellgrewe)

The Prussian gunboat *Arminius* at sea.

French Navy officer. (Drawing by Richard Knötel)

French Navy seaman. (Drawing by Richard Knötel)

French Marine infantryman. (Drawing by Richard Knötel)

Treatment of Prisoners

Shortly after the outbreak of the conflict, the flow of French prisoners to Germany began. The authorities considered themselves under an obligation to house them in a similar condition to that afforded to German soldiers in barracks. In the early stages this was accomplished by sending the French prisoners to fortresses throughout the German states where there was secure accommodation and a garrison capable of acting as guards. However, as the number of prisoners increased and the fortresses filled up, alternative sites had to be found. At first this consisted of huge camps with tents and huts. As winter approached the tents proved to be inadequate and some provision of heating the huts was made. Conditions for most of the prisoners was still miserable, despite the best efforts of the authorities and the donations made by many individual Germans, including visits to the sick and wounded by the Grand Duchess of Baden, who was the daughter of King Wilhelm of Prussia.

The 152 camps or depots set up in Northern Germany housed 10,700 officers and 305,000 NCOs and men; in the South German states, there were 43 depots with 1,100 officers and 66,600 NCOs and men. Each depot had a German army officer in command and to make accounting easier the prisoners were divided into companies of up to 300 men, later enlarged to 500 men or more. Officer prisoners were allowed to find and pay for private quarters on the condition that they gave their word not to escape. If they would not agree to these conditions, they and those who could not afford to pay were housed in officer's quarters within barracks or fortresses. Officer prisoners received a rate of pay from the German states according to their rank. The French Republican government also contributed a special allowance to each officer, but while the war continued it could not be paid directly and so had to be sent through a neutral agency – in this case the British Embassy in each of the German states. NCOs and men also received a small payment, but with deductions for food and clothing. Where possible the prisoners were encouraged to spend several hours each day working for the German military authorities without pay, but if they worked overtime they were entitled to extra pay. If they could find paid work from private individuals, this was encouraged.

The officially inspired relatively decent treatment of French prisoners contradicts the claim of brutality often aimed by later commentators. Despite the absence of any preparation for the huge numbers involved and the wintery conditions (the winter of 1870–1871 was one of the worst in living memory) the mortality rate remained low. In Bavaria 1,508 out of 39,339 prisoners died by mid-February 1871 (3.8 percent) and in the Prussian-controlled states of Germany, 7,230 out of 285,124 died (2.5 percent). These low percentages led to a positive review by a French delegation that had been allowed to inspect the camp conditions. Not only did the French prisoners initially have to face a lack of organisation, but poor food, inadequate accommodation, the lack of proper clothing to face the terrible winter conditions all took their toll. Many Prussian camp commanders took pains to alleviate the appalling conditions as best they could, albeit with limited resources.

The itinerary of a French priest who visited prison camps and hospitals in early 1871 bringing spiritual and physical comfort to French prisoners shows where and the numbers of prisoners housed. He kept an account of his journeys together with his trials and tribulations. In January 1871 he travelled to Bavaria and visited the prison camp at Ingolstadt and then according to his notes onward to:

Eichstadt citadel (prison) and hospital,
Ulm (in Wurttemberg) 1,000 French prisoners used as labourers at the fort,
Kienlesberg,
Wilhelmsberg, citadel used as a prisoner clearing station,
Stuttgart, French officers on parole living in private quarters,
Ludwigsburg, officers' camp in Hohenasperg Castle,
To Baden: Carlsruhe,
Rastadt, 9,000 prisoners, officers on parole in city (spent their time fishing in the River Murg), Accompanies the Countess Zeppelin on hospital visits, 150 officers and 2,000 men taken at Metz,
Cologne, 20,000 prisoners,
Heidelberg, one each hospital for officers and soldiers,
Mannheim, prisoners housed in wooden huts,
Darmstadt, 4,000 prisoners,
Mayence, 27,000 prisoners in wooden huts (outbreak of smallpox),
Frankfort-on-the-Main, French officers taken at Paris,
Coblentz, two camps, one with 10,000 men the other with 8,000,
Cologne (again) all French prisoners organised into companies and battalions each with Prussian officers, all wear a square of white canvas on the shoulders with their name and company number, depots at surrounding sites, Wahner-Heid, 4,000 men, Deutz, 2,000 men, Kalk, 3,000 men, Gremberg, 8,000 men,
Wiesbaden, French officers on parole including the wounded MacMahon (joined by his wife!),
Dusseldorf,
Neuss,
Wesel, 15,000 prisoners,
Minden,
Hanover (few prisoners as the Prussians did not trust the local population!),
The following towns along the Dutch border:
Telgte, 1,000 prisoners

Lingen, 3,000 [ditto]
Kellerberg, 2000 [ditto]
Papenburg, 2,000 [ditto]
Meppen, 1,000 [ditto]
Leer, 2,000 [ditto]
Emden, 1,000 [ditto]
then to Oldenburg and Bremen, 1000 prisoners
Magdeburg, 700 to 800 men in each of 36 companies.
Halberstadt, 400 officers (and their servants),
Blankenburg,
Wittenberg, 5,000 in huts with three hospitals for sick,
Halle, 500 sick plus ? prisoners working for locals,
Merseburg,
Weissenfels, 400 officers
Naumburg,
Torgau, 10 to 15,000 (small-pox outbreak), attempted escapes recorded. Issue to the prisoners of worn-out Prussian coats, boots and shoes,
Erfurt, 15,000 plus 500 officers,
Spandau, 10 depots in the camp each with 1,000 plus prisoners, three hospitals for the sick,
Stettin, 20 to 30,000 prisoners held in three forts, named 'Prussia', 'Wilhelm' and 'Leopold' and artillery barracks, parade ground with huts, 6,000 men in 'Polygon' fort, camps at Alt-Damm 4,000 men, sick sent to hospitals at Neustadt, Passewald and Stargard. French civilian prisoners used for forced labour,
Danzig, which had a population of 64,000 and 12,000 prisoners,
Konigsberg, 10,000,
Graudenz, 2,000,
Posen (General Steinmetz commander), Polish population sympathetic to French,
Gross-Glogau, 15,000 in huts barracks, stables and warehoused, five hospitals for typhus and dysentery plus separate hospital for small-pox,
Breslau,
Schweidnitz, 2,000,
Glatz, 4,000 prisoners, some dug a tunnel, a few escaped across border to Austria,
Neisse, 15,000 including civilians and the Mayor of Argenteuil (just to the northwest of Paris),
Cosel,
Dresden, 15,000 in camp at Ubigau, officers on parole in city, fort of Konigstein,
Leipzig, 2,000

It seems that all French prisoners were organised, taking their example from Cologne, into numbered companies with German officers.

Women in the War

It was accepted that women would play a role as nurses, or generally assisting the wounded – though not by all as many officials still insisted on doctors and nurses being male. However, there were other ways in which women patriotically supported their country: everything from carrying a weapon in the ranks of the volunteers to an artist living near Paris who refused to share her dining table with Prussian officers billeted in her house.

The story of Juliette Dodu is almost in the realms of legend, at the time of the German occupation of Pithivers she ran the post and telegraph office, which was seized, and the family forced to live on the second floor of the building. Juliette had manged to secrete a telegraph receiver and rigged up a tap on the wire with which she intercepted incoming and outgoing messages sent by the Germans. For nearly three weeks she passed on the messages to the French authorities without suspicion until a German soldier overheard a conversation between members of the household. Juliette was arrested and brought before a court martial accused of spying. She was found guilty and condemned to death, but fortunately the armistice was signed before sentence could be carried out. Her story was published in the newspaper *Le Figaro* in May 1877 and she was awarded the Military Medal and the Cross of the Legion of Honour. It may just have been a story cooked up by the paper to promote French 'heroines' in the years after the war. She later met Felix Larrey, chief medical officer of the French Army, the son of Napoleon I's personal doctor and ultimately inherited his fortune and estate. She became a government official and inspector of schools and asylums.

Marie-Antoinette Lix was born in Colmar, Haut-Rhin, Alsace, France to François-Antoine Lix and Françoise Schmitt in 1839. She was given a full military education by her father, who later sent her to Sisters of Divine Providence in Ribeauvillé to be further educated. After graduating as a teacher, she became a governess with a Polish noble family in Szycz. She joined the Polish insurrection against Russia in 1863 and acted as a courier on the side of the Polish rebels but was captured by the Russians and later released. She returned to France in 1866. Following the Battle of Sedan, Lix joined the French Army under General Pierre de Failly. She joined the Volunteers of Lamarche as a lieutenant. She participated in the defence of the Vosges area and the city of Langres and distinguished herself during the Battle of Nompatelize on 6 October 1870. She died in 1909 in Saint-Nicolas-de-Port, Meurthe-et-Moselle. In 1910, an organisation of women of Strasbourg and Colmar donated a silver sword in her honour to the *Musée de l'Armée* in Paris.

Marie Favier-Nicolaï (born Marie Eugénie Demigneux in 1843) was another of the women who took part in the 1870 war as a combatant. Attached to the Army of the Vosges, she was part of the command of Giuseppe Garibaldi and served in the Nicolaï Battalion. On 15 December 1870, in Autun, Captain Banet offered her a sword in the name of all the officers of the battalion as a mark of the respect they had for this courageous woman. She later became capitain-adjudant-major of the *Francs-Tireurs* of The Doubs.

Chapter 3

Germany

> Every able-bodied man, according to most correspondents, then donned his uniform and shouldered his rifle, or bestrode his horse; all kind of business was at a standstill: factories were closed, shops shut up, crops left on the fields uncut; all production was stopped, all commerce abandoned – in fact, it was a case of 'suspended animation', a tremendous national effort, but which, if prolonged only a few months, must end in complete national exhaustion. The transformation of civilians into soldiers did certainly go on at a rate of which people out of Germany had no idea; but if the same writers will look at Germany now, after the withdrawal of above a million men from civil life, they will find the factories working, the crops housed, the shops and counting-houses open. Production, if stopped at all, is stopped for want of orders, not for want of hands; and there are plenty of stout fellows to be seen about the streets quite as fit to shoulder a rifle as those who have gone off to France.

So wrote Frederick Engels in *The Pall Mall Gazette* of 8 October 1870.[1] So, what was the system whereby the army could be brought up to full strength, with its losses replaced, and the economy continue to function more or less as normal?

The war between France and Prussia and her allies had been engineered by King Wilhelm's first minister, Bismarck, as part of his overall aim of uniting Germany under the rule of the Prussian monarchy. He had been aided by France's political system under which Napoleon III had been dictator since his *coup d'état* in December 1851. By 1869 he was a sick man and decided to reform his government as a 'liberal empire', passing some of the decisions of state to his ministers. Unfortunately, this did not lead to a particularly stable administration, and led instead to agitation from liberals and radicals for a greater share of government.

Bismarck had been aided by the Prussian Minister of War, General Albrecht von Roon, who had been an advocate for the reform of the army which he had largely carried through. He had commanded troops in action and been a senior figure in the Great General Staff.

The third member of the group was General Helmuth von Moltke, head and guiding hand of the Great General Staff, who had devised successful plans for the war against Denmark in 1864, Austria and the German states in 1866, and assured Bismarck that the army could beat the French.

---

1 Frederick Engels, 'The Rationale of the Prussian Army System', *Pall Mall Gazette*, 8 October 1870.

Prussian infantry column on the march, winter 1870-71. (Watercolour by Maurice Toussaint)

Prussian hussars skirmishing. (Watercolour by Maurice Toussaint)

Intelligence Services and Spies

In planning for the war against Austria, Moltke set up an intelligence office within the Great General Staff to gather information on Austrian military capabilities. This office existed until the end of the First World War spreading its remit to cover all prospective enemy countries. In 1867 he set up another office to gather readily available information, now known as 'open source' information, on other countries. This geographic and statistical office was similar to those organised by other countries. In Britain the 'Topographical Depot' was in existence by 1860.

Bismarck also had other means at his disposal to give him the confidence to take on what was considered at the time to be the greatest military power in Europe. He had his own intelligence service, run by a Berlin policeman called Wilhelm Stieber. Originally intended for the church, propelled by his father,

Prussians tapping the French telegraph. (*The Graphic*)

a Lutheran minister and his mother, an English lady named Daisy Cromwell (reputably a descendant of Oliver Cromwell), Stieber had rebelled against the family wishes and instead studied law at the university in Berlin. When his father found out, he cut off his funding. To pay for his further studies Stieber took a job with the police and became an Inspector with the Criminal Division. So successfully did he pursue his duties that after the attempted revolution in Berlin in 1848, a grateful king, Frederick William IV, made him Chief of Police of the Prussian capital. As a result, he soon came to Bismarck's attention.

After the war of 1866 against Austria, Bismarck foresaw that Prussia would have to tackle France at some time in the future and used Stieber as his agent to find information on new French weapons, the Chassepot rifle and the *Mitrailleuse.* He reported back that they were no means as formidable as feared. While in Paris he posed as a journalist named Schmidt and began to set up a network of agents prepared to sell information (through Bismarck he had access to large amounts of cash). He chose men who were in debt, or otherwise disgruntled with the French government. His staff in Berlin kept detailed records on anybody and everybody who could be useful, given the right inducements, including blackmail.

Several of the major espionage coups were performed by an agent Stieber identified only by the initials 'FM'. This agent reputedly contacted and recruited a group of elite spies, all high-ranking opponents of the French emperor Napoleon III. Stieber gave FM a free hand in running these spies and was rewarded with faith in the agent's abilities when FM gained a copy of the French Army's deployment plans in the event of a war with Prussia. Having learned the location of these plans, FM obtained them by posing as a decorator and bluffing his way into the War Ministry with a ladder and a tin of paint. Once in the room, FM set up his tools and made a copy of the plans in between decorating the walls.

When the war eventually broke out Stieber had his agents in place to provide Bismarck with much useful information. He was also given the task of organising a field security police force to protect the king and his senior staff on campaign. He was given responsibility to gather information on the French Army in the field, to seek out any French spies and check on the members of the press who swarmed into the battle zones and rear areas. 'Spy mania' was everywhere and every civilian was treated as an enemy agent unless they could produce the right papers and prove otherwise. Stieber's agents even supervised the postal service and had the power to censor sensitive information.

Stieber would evaluate the information his organisation had gathered and twice weekly make a report to the king. He even had an agent on Marshal McMahon's staff who reported that Napoleon was still with the army in Sedan, when everyone else had assumed that he had made his escape. During the siege of Paris, the German headquarters at Versailles was under Stieber's direct protection, with his secret police agents keeping everything and everybody under surveillance.

More decisive was Stieber's investigation on secret communications between Versailles and Paris. His spies tracked down an extensive system of underground passages that were being used to supply Paris with food. Every night up to 300 wagons passed through these tunnels with their wheels wrapped in cloth to prevent them making a noise. This discovery explained spy reports from inside the city that Paris had ample provisions for a siege. Stieber reported his findings to Bismarck, also pointing out that morale at home was plummeting because of the stalemate. With no end to the siege in sight, the decision to bombard Paris was eventually taken. Until then the Prussians had refrained from indiscriminate firing on the city, but when they did results were almost instantaneous. After 5 January Prussian heavy artillery fired 10,000 shells into the city, destroying over 200 buildings. Stieber's spies in the city reported that the storehouses had burned, and people were killing cats and dogs for meat – they even reported the establishment of a rat market.

On the night of 23/24 January, Stieber's agents inside Paris reported that a high-ranking person was coming out to negotiate. Stieber galloped back to his quarters and arranged to host the expected negotiations. After disguising his agents in civilian clothes, he prepared overnight lodgings for the French. 'We lit a good fire,' he wrote, 'prepared two beds and, as the French believed that, like Versailles, we were dying of hunger, I did everything possible to procure some good food, desserts, pastries and so on.'[2] When the vice-president, Jules Favre, arrived at Stieber's lodgings to spend the night, he had his agents watch him, spying on Favre through a hole in the wall.

Prussian Command System

History has shown that armies in all sorts of conditions can win great victories against seemingly impossible odds, provided they are led by a general of genius. Napoleon I during his career is a good example, as are the Duke of Wellington and the Russian Suvorov and Gustavus Adolphus of Sweden. These generals could

2 Wilhelm J.C.E. Stieber, The Chancellor's Spy (New York: Grove Press, 1979)

lead troops, arrange resources and make political decisions as needed. General von Moltke did not consider himself in the same class but realised early on that there was no guarantee that such a genius would appear when needed. His conclusion was that a 'corporate genius' could do the job and the development of the Prussian Great General Staff was the result, which had actually been formed by Scharnhorst, Gneisenau and Clausewitz after the Napoleonic Wars. Much has been written on this body and numerous studies have been undertaken, from the time of the conflict to the present day. Moltke was not a battle-hardened leader, having only limited practical experience, when he was seconded to the Turkish Army and employed during the Syrian campaign which led to the Battle of Nisib between an Egyptian army and the Ottoman Turks. He had advised the Ottoman commander on the best course of action, which had been duly ignored, with disastrous results. (The Egyptians had followed the advice of a French Army officer and won the battle.)

The Prussian system of army command was based on Napoleonic originals with corps and armies under a royal prince or a general from the aristocracy. Moltke could not replace this aristocratic system, but if he could place an officer whom he had trained into the headquarters of large formations he could exercise virtual control. The permanent personnel of the Great General Staff was quite small – for example, just 13 officers in the 1870 campaign – but each year a selection of officers who had attended the War Academy were taken under Moltke's guidance and inculcated with his ideas. These would serve a term with the Staff and then return to their old units to keep up with current practice, then come back to the Staff for more training before being allocated to a senior officer as his chief of staff. Orders issued by the king of Prussia as supreme chief were sent to army and corps commanders, until Moltke eventually got permission to issue orders for a senior formation direct to the corps commander and to his own nominee, the chief of staff, who exercised executive command in the field, albeit not always successfully.

Unusual view of a Prussian artillery unit, note the gunners marching on foot. (*Illustrated London News*)

Prussian officers' quarters at an outpost during the siege of Paris. (*Illustrated London News*)

The 'corporate command' of senior commander and his chief of staff was intended, by Moltke, to receive his orders, formulate a plan of action, following his directions, and come to an agreement. General Steinmetz deliberately ignored his chief of staff (and Moltke), while the Prussian crown prince and his chief of staff, General Blumenthal, worked as an effective team. When the Prussian Army set off for Bohemia in June 1866, King William issued an order that was to make history. It decreed that 'from now on my orders concerning the operational movements of the concentrated army and its individual parts shall be communicated to the commands through the chief of the general staff of the army'.

The Great General Staff had several departments and functions, all further developed by Moltke once he had gained the confidence of the Prussian king. The Historical Section studied and published accounts of former campaigns. Moltke considered that officers should study military history as it had equal importance with strategy, as well as map understanding, languages, geography and troop leading. Another function was to formulate plans against any possible contingency and have them continuously updated. Full use was made of modern innovations, planning railway timetables became an art and the telegraph enabled orders and information to be transmitted with lightning speed (although mounted aides de camp were still necessary on the battlefield). The Great General Staff was directly subordinate to the king of Prussia and was independent of the War Ministry.

After the war of 1866, Bavaria organised a General Staff of its own on basically similar lines but subordinated to the Minister of War.

Moltke developed the revolutionary idea (for 1870) of issuing orders as brief 'directives', telling the recipient the general plan of the forthcoming action and leaving the detail of the army or corps movements to its commander and his chief of staff. This gave considerable latitude to generals to devise their own actions as long as they conformed with the overall idea transmitted by Moltke. Staff officers would advise or even overrule the senior commander if they felt that the plan was not being adhered to. This caused problems if a Steinmetz decided he knew better and marched off in a different direction (as at Saarbrucken and Gravelotte), or a Prince Frederick Charles wanted to argue the plan. The system worked well as long as the army/corps/division generals knew the plan and what was in Moltke's mind as explained by the chief of staff of the formation. The years that Moltke had spent training his Great General Staff officers now bore fruit. Unlike the French command system, where the emperor and army commanders did not communicate their intentions to their subordinates, the senior Prussian leaders all were made aware of what was expected of them. This led to the Prussian principle of 'marching to the sound of the guns' without waiting for express orders to do so. (Though not always in the right direction.) The General Staff order to engage in a major battle could consist of a single sheet of paper stating the overall plan, the 'directive', and a unit's orders could be just a few lines long. It was almost as if Moltke said, the enemy is at point X, get there via point Y and attack him. However, the technology of the day, the railway and the field telegraph organisation still meant that in the last resort a mounted messenger with a piece of paper in his pocket, or a staff officer with a verbal message, was the only way of transmitting orders on the battlefield itself. This seems fairly basic by modern standards, but at the time was revolutionary. No other country came close to this level of professionalism: the French had a staff corps, but without a permanent organisation; the Russians and Austrians kept their general staff departments within their respective war offices; and the British and American armies had no staff worthy of the name. This did not give the Prussians the absolute assurance of winning a war, but it did give them an overwhelming advantage that they were not slow to exploit.

A Prussian army telegraph unit deploy their equipment.

The following remarks on the Prussian Army in the field were written by Brigadier-General Hazen,[3] US Army, quartered with the Prussian crown prince's army at Paris.

> Prussian equipment
> The Prussian soldier has his overcoat made into a long slender roll, and hung on the left shoulder, the two ends coming together, and being fastened on the right hip. His haversack of coarse white linen, and a glass canteen covered with leather, are slung from the right shoulder.
>
> Around the flask are buckled two broad straps, used in peace to cover the sights of the gun. He wears no cross-belts, but a pipe-clayed waist-belt, on which are slipped two cartridge-boxes of black leather, carried on either side, each box holding twenty. The knapsack is made of calf-skin and is slung by two leather straps hooked to the waist-belt in front and then passing over the shoulders. Two short straps attached to these in front pass back under the armpits and are fastened to the knapsack. The knapsack is made to keep its shape by a light wooden frame, and the leather is flint-tanned, or stretched over this frame while green. On each end outside is a deep box, in which is carried a case of twenty cartridges.

3 Hazen's notes were based on his direct observations in the field, and were intended for an American audience, both military and domestic. Comparisons are made with the organisation and arms and equipment of the American forces of the time. Hazen was an experienced officer who had held a senior command during the Civil War and afterward.

Within are one shirt of white flannel, one pair of drawers, one pair of drill trousers, a short drill jacket, one pair of boots, and the cleaning and toilet kit, consisting of four or five brushes for the clothes, hair, teeth, gun, blacking and polishing; then a box of pumice-stone, a bottle of sweet-oil, and the usual quantity of old greasy rags for cleaning. –

In addition to this, the soldier carries writing material and a roll of bandages. On top of his knapsack is strapped a galvanized iron pot, holding about three quarts, with a tight-fitting cover, which is used separately for cooking. Within the knapsack, slipped into little loops, are a spoon, knife, fork, comb, and small mirror. The latter does not seem to be required, but is permitted. In his haversack is carried whatever may be the food for the day. He wears a single-breasted frock-coat of blue cloth with red facings, very dark grey pantaloons, short top-boots, and no stockings. He wears on his waist-belt a strong sword fifteen inches long, which he can use for defence, and for cutting wood, or material for fascines or gabions. His gun is unburnished, so that it may not attract the enemy by flashing in the sun, and is pretty well coated with grease. He carries no blanket, but hopes at night to find some straw for his bed. He wears on his head either a flat forage-cap with red band, or the peaked helmet. Carrying the inspection farther, you find that the soldier answers to the question 'When did you bathe last?' 'When at home, I bathe daily from May till September, but I have not bathed at all since leaving Germany.'

A leather pouch for money is hung about the neck, and also a zinc plate attached to a card, on which are engraved the soldier's regiment, company, and number. The whole weight of the soldier's arms and equipment is fifty pounds [22½kg.]. He pays for his mess the cost of it, on a peace-footing, comes out of his daily pay, which is three and one-half silver groschen, or about two pence in money, [but with the purchasing power of £2 today.] He is allowed, besides, a pound and a half of rye bread. Excepting the bread, the ration is not fixed in kind, but is determined by a board of officers, and varies with the products and prices of localities.

The companies are divided into messes of about twenty men, each of which is under the charge of a non-commissioned officer. Each company has its mess-board, composed of the captain, a lieutenant, a non-commissioned officer, and some privates, who decide all questions pertaining to themselves, regulate the bills of fare, and determine the daily cost to each soldier, and the hours of meals. The bill of fare varies greatly with localities. Usually, in Germany, the breakfast consists of a thin flour soup, with some slices of bread; the dinner, of meat, generally mutton, or beef and vegetables; the supper, of what happens to remain over. Coffee or tea is usually had once a day, although not considered a part of the ration. But while in active service, each man receives a good ration of bread and meat, with coffee and wine, or whatever the country supplies. The daily cost rarely exceeds two silver groschen, and with this an abundance of vegetables is provided, in addition to meat and bread. At stated intervals, say once in two or three days, the cost of messes is collected, and the little leather bag suspended about the neck is inspected, to see if the money has been foolishly expended.

Uniform clothing

There are three suits of clothing for each soldier. The suit for everyday he turns in when he has permission to go to town, and dresses neatly for his holiday. He turns in his common suit on Saturday, and is given the one for Sunday. He has still another, brought out only on great occasions, such as royal reviews. The clothing is kept by the first Sergeant, and although, on the average, a suit lasts only a year, each of the old suits being degraded one degree in importance when a new one is issued, it is not uncommon to find suits in stock that have been in service twenty years. The foregoing arrangement applies, of course, only to garrison life; and when the army takes the field only one suit is worn; but a marvellous faculty for brushing up enables the men to come out on occasions of ceremony as neat and glittering as though just from the wardrobe of the barrack. The soldier is besides allowed annually two pairs of cotton drawers, two shirts of the same, and two pairs of boots. He also has each year one white cotton cloth suit for drilling, and two black-cloth stocks. The stock is worn by all grades, no one using white collars.

Officer's dress
The officers receive a reasonable pay, and pay for their own clothes themselves, and the most scrupulous care of their personal appearance is expected. Their dress is so like that of the privates, that but for its texture, and the shoulder-straps and swords, one can scarcely distinguish them from the common soldiers. The have three distinct dresses. Full dress is a single-breasted frock-coat with one row of buttons, sword, sash, and helmet, and corded black pantaloons. Dress nearly full, corresponding to the dress-coat and black cravat of a civilian, is a coat like the first, except that it is double-breasted, and has two rows of buttons, with the same pantaloons, sword, sash, and helmet. The fatigue dress is the last-described coat and pantaloons, with the forage-cap in place of the helmet. This corresponds to the morning-dress of a civilian. There is, besides this, the working-suit, answering to the drill jacket and pantaloons of the men.

The most scrupulous deference is always paid to superiors in rank; and many regulations seem, quite absurd. For example, officers are not allowed to carry an umbrella or bundles. If walking with a lady while shopping, an officer could not carry her parcel.

Army police
Every corps has 40 picked men, who serve as gendarmes, or army-police. They are mounted, armed with sabres and revolvers, and uniformed much like cavalry, only that the colour of the coat is green. Each man wears about his neck a metal chain with a plate in front, on which is his number. They receive orders only from general officers, and in their own proper sphere are obeyed by all below that grade.

Soldier's pay
The soldiers receive their pay every ten days; although those who spend it, and have nothing left for their mess costs, are paid daily. Then, if they fail to save for their mess, the pay is given to a non-commissioned officer, who uses enough for this purpose, and hands the remainder to the soldier. Each soldier is allowed six cigars a day, which cost him but one silver groschen. He is responsible for his arms and equipment; and if any are lost by his fault, the loss is made up by the company, if he has previously been of a good character; otherwise he must pay.

The field telegraph
The Prussian army adapted the electric telegraph to field purposes. The system is based on the Morse code. Each head-quarters of an army and each army corps has a telegraphic division of three officers, 137 men, 73 horses, and ten wagons. Two of the latter are fitted up as operating rooms, and the other eight are used for carrying poles and other material, including five miles [8 km] of wire to each wagon, which can be reeled off by the moving of the vehicle. Of the whole forty miles [64 km], five are insulated, and can be run along the ground. It will be seen that each army corps can put out forty miles [64 km] of line without recourse to other wires, but use is always made of lines found in the country, if they will answer. Single poles of light material are used, without joints, and about ten feet [3.5 m] long, and only every third pole is put in the ground. The personnel are recruited into the army from the civil telegraphic service at home. While in the field, the operators assume military rank, and, like agents of the Post-office Department, are known as 'military officials,' not as 'military officers.' The men are on a footing with train-soldiers, and all wear a distinctive emblem on the tunic. The carriages are painted of a dark olive-brown, and are

each drawn by four horses. Just in rear of the driver is a partition shutting off the rear portion of the carriage. At his back, and under his seat, is a capacious box, in which are carried tools, and the material necessary in telegraphing. On one side of the rear closed portion is a table, with an operating instrument on it, and the battery under it; and on the opposite side is the operator's bench, the space underneath it being also used for equipment. On the outside, near the table, are sockets, with thumb-screws connected with the battery, to which the wires are fitted. The king is connected with his ministers, and lines are also run from General von Moltke's headquarters to all of the different corps in the field.

The Germans also used a semaphore system with a mast, and with flags displayed at different heights. The telegraph corps is fully mobile to keep up with the army as it moves forward.

The Field Post

The personnel belonging to the Field Post are brought from the civil mail service, and is upon the same footing with the telegraph corps. Each brigade, division, corps, and army, as well as the king and his ministers, has its own special service, its own officers, and the principal personages have their own post bags. The post is received daily at the terminus of the railway and are delivered to officers of the postal service for the various parts of the army. In the 1866 campaign many wounded soldiers looked for the postal service first, to send news home, before waiting to be picked up by the ambulance troops.

Bavarian infantry moving to the attack, showing an array of extemporized winter clothing!
(Drawing by Richard Knötel)

A New German Army: The *Etappen*

The '*Etappen*' roughly translates as 'the lines of communication' and was a separate army organisation with responsibility for the occupied parts of France, for security in the towns and villages, maintenance of roads and railways and bridges. It had to be organised immediately the campaign began as the field armies moved into France and opened a gap between the fighting troops and the homeland. Some regular troops were used together with reservists and *Landwehr* men, both infantry and cavalry and some lightly wounded and convalescents. If the situation demanded it, sections of artillery were seconded from the field armies.

The *Etappen* duties included: resupply of all needs of the army; return of all material leaving the army (which included people and horses); accommodation and food for soldiers and animals; maintenance and security of all supply routes; manufacture and operation of light railways (in siege operations); and organisation and management of occupied areas.

The individual supply lines were organised by special inspectors. The supply lines were divided into districts in which supply command offices were set up. The army assigned the officers, civil servants (many of the administration specialists, such as railway engineers) and soldiers required to these supply command offices.

At the head of the entire staging system of an army was the general inspector of the communication and railroad system. He was also in charge of all railway troops, the field directorate, the field medical service, the field telegraph, and the field postal system.

The commander of this army had an enormous task before him, including the supply of three, later four armies in the field, the supervision of the occupied areas of France through which these supplies had to travel, the protection of the roads and railways which carried the traffic in an unceasing flow throughout the war. The man chosen was little known among the mass of the Prussian Army at the time and is barely remembered today. General Albrecht von Stosch came from a military family and had slowly worked his way up through the army, entering as a cadet in 1832. He served as a company officer and later in the capacity of staff officer in various corps throughout Prussia. However, he had come to the notice of Moltke, who regarded him as a man of intelligence, skill and determination. He had been on the staff of the crown prince during the 1866 campaign in Bohemia and gained the confidence of many officers on the Great General Staff. After the campaign he was appointed to a post in the Ministry of War, where he gained experience in military economics. He had hoped for an active command in 1870 and was disappointed at first with the post of Intendant General, consoled by the fact that both Moltke (Chief of the Great General Staff and effectively commander of the North German Army and of the southern states) and Roon (the Minister of War) were convinced that he was the best man for the job. The crown prince of Prussia even put in a request that he be sent to his headquarters as his chief of staff.

In the opening weeks of the war, the field of operations was expected to be the border areas, the German Rhineland and the French districts of Alsace and Lorraine. Once the French Army had been defeated (there was no doubt in the mind of the Chief of the General Staff that this would the case), the armies would march on Paris and dictate terms to the French emperor, or whatever government existed. This had been the scenario in 1815 at the outset of the '100 Days' and the Prussian (and Austrian and Russian and British) armies would live off the land, France being a largely agricultural country and the summer being a time of plenty. This was, perhaps, Moltke's greatest error of judgement. In all his preparations the scenario was that the French Army would be defeated, and the possibility that France would choose to fight on had not been considered. While the German armies surrounded and blockaded Paris (with the curious situation that they were out-numbered by the defenders) and other armies fought against the French Army of the Loire and the French Army of the North and later the French Army of the East, the occupied areas had to be defended and supplies from Germany had to be protected from official and unofficial bands of volunteer *francs-tireurs*.

The *Etappen* army was not a regular force, but was made up *Landwehr* units, reservists and lightly wounded convalescent soldiers who had not yet returned to their parent units. A few regulars were added where necessary, along with some cavalry squadrons and artillery batteries. As the situation changed in the field, the composition of the *Etappen* army also changed.

However, in 1870, the armies were considerably larger than in 1815 and after the Battle of Sedan and the later surrender of Metz, the Prussians had not only to feed their own troops, but they also had to provide for masses of prisoners. It is true that Sedan and Metz had yielded vast amounts of stores as had other French depots in the border areas, but not enough to cope with the situation. And as the German armies marched through the countryside to Paris, supply lines were stretched to breaking point. Food, for man and beast, had to be procured daily and ammunition had to be brought up to refill the soldier's pouches and the artillery limbers. All the other necessities of war had to be provided; the constant cry from the company and regimental officers was for boots, as the soldier's footwear quickly fell to pieces on the long marches, even more speedily as the summer turned to autumn and then to winter. The French did not help matters by breaking up roads, destroying rail lines, blowing up bridges and blocking railway tunnels.

The *Etappen* columns used wagons, country carts, whatever they could bring from Germany or commandeer from France and the beasts to pull them. Where railways were in working order, they were quickly brought into operation. Hundreds of French railway trucks but only about 50 locomotives were captured and put to use, with 3,600 railway personnel brought in from the state railway companies of Germany. The transport services took 280 locomotives from the German railways companies and a further 75 were purchased.

The conquered areas of France were divided into several areas or 'governments', each with its military compliment, depending on the tasks allotted to it. With the siege of Paris commencing in the middle of September of 1870, and with German armies facing new French formations in the Loire Valley and in the north – all of which needed the attention of the regular troops – the *Landwehr* was given the role of guarding the lines of communication.

After the fall of Metz on 27 October the garrison and *Etappen* troops were reorganised. The garrison troops were allocated to the three governments. The government of Alsace, under Lieutenant-General Count Bismarck-Bohlen, had in its command 23 infantry battalions, nine cavalry squadrons and two-and-a-half batteries of artillery; the government of Lorraine, under General von Bonin, had 20 infantry battalions, six cavalry squadrons and two batteries of artillery; and the government of Rheims, under the Grand-Duke of Mecklenburg-Schwerin, had 17 battalions of infantry, four squadrons of cavalry and three batteries of artillery. The *Etappen* troops were distributed with one battalion of infantry and one squadron of cavalry to the German 1st Army; four battalions and two squadrons to the 2nd Army; 16 battalions and nine squadrons to the 3rd Army; and four battalions and two squadrons to the Army of the Meuse. The total number of these 'second line' troops was 85 battalions of infantry, 33 squadrons of cavalry and nine-and-a-half batteries of artillery. On 16 December a fourth 'government' was formed, based at Versailles, under General von Fabrice.

The battalions were generally composed of six companies, each of 200 men.

The occupation of French territory was placed under the orders of a Governor General. This officer was given strict instructions by the king of Prussia on how to carry out his duties. He was given full powers over the civilian and military authorities, but the king admonished him to 'act with forbearance towards the inhabitants'. The Governor General was to take full control of his area and ensure that no French officials exercised any former authority. He was to raise any taxes necessary to support his administration and customary police duties. French laws were to be continued by the local courts. The Governor General had control of the postal, telegraph and railway communications and the power to stop any part of it if necessary. He had to provide an account to the king on the 1st and 15th of each month.

Prussian Landwehr. (Watercolour by Maurice Toussaint)

Reserve Officers

As well as a vast number of men needed to fill the ranks of the army and *Landwehr*, to guard the lines of communication, to maintain roads, railways in the occupied areas of France and to provide security for the enormous crowds of prisoners, suitable officers were needed to command them. The Germans resolved this problem by recalling retired officers and those who had left the service, provided they were still capable of serving in the field. To augment this number further men were commissioned who had originally been enlisted men who had distinguished service in the face of the enemy in previous wars. Former one- and three-year volunteers who had attained the position of *Portepee-Fahnriche* and who had a certificate that they were qualified as officers were called up. A number of enlisted men who had also gained the certificate of qualification on leaving the service were also called. They were generally assigned to the branch of the service in which they had formerly served.

The reserve officers were clothed in the uniform of their former units but were distinguished by the addition of the *Landwehr* cross in silver to their headgear. As the infantry helmet plate had the royal monogram (FR or FWR) on the breast of the eagle the cross was fitted just below it. On the guard regiments the cross was fitted over the silver 'guard star', but in yellow metal. The guard grenadier eagle had the cross fitted to the eagle's breast. The same went for cavalry helmets, the hussars had the cross fitted to the front of the fur cap, except the Life Hussars numbers 1 and 2, where it was fitted at the right side, so as not to obscure the Death's Head plate.

Commissariat

The amount of supplies needed by the German armies was enormous. Each corps had its local recruiting area and this was the basis of its supply sources. The army's needs were collected in their local districts and forward by rail as far as possible. Local products were supplemented by orders placed abroad. A contract sent to England for 3 million lbs (1.36 million kg) of preserved meat with the same amount of biscuit and compressed forage was to be delivered to Cologne. Once on French soil the Germans were determined that local resources would support their armies, even by offering to pay for food and fodder as well as by forced requisitions, but only about a third of what was needed was forthcoming. The Commissariat had to supply the bulk. Large magazines were established along the lines of the railways, which were constantly refilled as the corps drew their supplies from them. A reserve of six weeks supply was built up at cities on the German side of the Rhine. Of course, as soon as the campaign began, with the German armies now across the frontier, the means of transport from the magazines to the troops initially proved inadequate. The capture of large stocks of food and forage that the French Army had assembled for their advance into Germany eased the situation slightly.

In the cities of Cologne, Coblenz, Bingen, Mainz, and Saarlouis 20 field ovens were built to supply the troops with bread. Further bakeries were set up in suitable buildings at Frankfurt-am-Main and Mannheim, the government flour stores providing the ingredients. Bakeries at the magazines on the railways were also enlarged and between them not only were the immediate requirements of the armies satisfied, but also a reserve of the ubiquitous biscuit. Fortunately, the army ration bread could stay edible for a few days before it went hard and stale but could always be revived by dunking into the soldiers' pea sausage soup.[4]

As the German armies advanced into France, new magazines were set up on French territory along the lines of intact railways. Although protected against the weather, considerable amounts of stores were damaged during the heavy rains of August. Even so, after the Battle of Gravelotte, the troops could not be supplied from the magazines or advanced stores and had to be given what the commissariat could get hold of – captured coffee and local wine.[5] Wine was also supplied in lieu of drinking water, where it could not be supplied in sufficient quantity locally, as many wells and streams were polluted. The Prussian Army had foreseen this problem and had equipped themselves with large numbers of 'Norton Tubes', an American invention of an iron pipe, made in sections, which could be pushed into the ground down to the water table. Unfortunately, the ground near the initial fighting was hard chalk and was difficult to penetrate. Supply columns of the French Army were captured and quickly made available to the German troops. The Prussian Guard Corps captured a French convoy containing enough food for seven days. It was not all one-way traffic, however. When the Prussian Army turned north in the attempt to take MacMahon in the flank, the message to change direction did not reach all the provision columns in time and one marched

4 A special ration made of dried peas, bacon, pork fat and spices. It was produced in a government factory in Berlin and issued in a dried sausage shape which could be cut into pieces and dropped into boiling water to make the basis of a soup or stew.

5 This did not mean that the troops were permanently inebriated, the alcohol content of wine was less than today. A modern beer has an alcohol content of 3%, or at most 4%. In 1870 it was no more than 1%. This was down to the brewing process and the low efficiency of the brewers' fermentation vessels.

Waggoners of German provision trains at Versailles. (*Illustrated London News*)

straight into the hands of the French. Local produce was also gathered to augment the requisitions by forced contributions. During the campaign the bumper potato and bean harvest in the occupied areas was collected directly by the Germans and lasted through the winter.

Some idea of the nightmare faced by the Commissariat was the daily requirements of the armies investing Paris. These included: 148,000 large (3 lb/1.4 kg) loaves of bread; 102,000 lbs (46,250 kg) of rice; 539 oxen or 102,000 lbs (46,250 kg) of bacon; 14,000 lbs (6,350 kg) of salt; 900,000 lbs (408,000 kg) of oats; 2,400,000 lbs (1,088,620 kg) of hay and 28,000 quarts (31,822 litres) of spirits. In addition, the troops were issued with an enormous quantity of coffee and sugar and huge numbers of cigars of different qualities. The amount of tobacco consumed was immense; at the time smoking was looked upon as beneficial for the troops. Even illustrations of troops on the march show nearly every man with a pipe between his lips, or on a cord dangling from a tunic button. Cigars were either of good quality for officers, or 'ordinary quality' for other ranks.

A Prussian Train column. (Drawing by Ernst Zimmer)

German field intendants. (Drawing by Ernst Zimmer)

Transport by rail was largely well organised by the commissariat, but the onward transmission from the railheads to the troops was by wagon and horses. Initially this was by impressing local famers and their carts, although they were paid and sometimes clothed. The work was not pleasant, and desertion was a big problem. The Germans tried to solve the problem by buying wagons and horses in Germany to be driven by men of the *Landwehr*. However, it was put into practice too late to affect the local transport situation before the war ended. The strain put on the army train can be seen from the records of the Prussian First Army: at the beginning of the war, it had 2,000 wagons but by the middle of October could find barely 20.

After the fall of Metz, the German 2nd Army was sent to Orleans to support the troops facing the French Army of the Loire. It was supported by its own transport columns which were kept filled from magazines especially established for them and through the expedient of carrying large amounts of cash with which to buy food and fodder from the inhabitants of the country districts through which they passed. By the judicious use of a published tariff setting out prices they would pay and threatening requisitions if the locals did not sell supplies, the troops were largely satisfied.

Prussian Infantry

The Battle of Gravelotte, although a victory for German (Prussian, Saxon and Hessian) armies, was catastrophic from the point of view of the Prussian nobility. The casualties suffered by the Germans were horrific not just in numbers but in the Prussian Guard, especially as the numbers of officers killed and wounded left almost every noble house mourning the loss of one or more members. The Guard Corps had gone into action approximately 18,000 men strong and had suffered the loss of 8,000 in killed, wounded and missing. The troops had marched against French infantry who opened a heavy fire, first at long range and, as they approached the enemy's position, the range shortened, and casualties mounted. The Guard Schutzen Battalion entered the action with 700 officers and men; by the end of the day 19 officers and 431 men were either killed or wounded. Among those killed were a Count zu Dohna, a Count von Schlieffen and a Baron von Buddenbrock; among the wounded were a Von Hindenburg, a Von der Knesebeck and another Count zu Dohna. Even the assistant surgeon killed in the battle was a Von Lichtenstein.

Why did the Germans and particularly the Guards suffer such horrendous casualties? A combination of outdated tactics at the battalion level saw the companies forming up behind each other in masses which the Chassepots could hardly miss. Another error was at the divisional level: the basic tactic should have been to plaster the French positions with artillery fire, but the infantry had moved off before the batteries were in position. The Prussian king was aghast when he saw the casualty lists and issued the following order:

> I have gathered from the reports on the detail of the recent victorious combats (Battle of Gravelotte) that the serious losses arose partly from the fact that the troops frequently advanced to the assault in battalion columns following too closely on their skirmishers.
>
> I therefore point out the fact that the assault on a hostile position must in the first instance be sufficiently prepared by the artillery and a well-directed fire of skirmishers; and that in the infrequent cases when turning or outflanking the enemy is not possible, and a frontal attack over open ground is therefore absolutely necessary, the formation of company columns and half battalions, as laid down by regulation and applied on the practice ground, must be employed.
>
> I bestow the fullest acknowledgment on the gallant forwardness of the infantry, to whom hitherto nothing has been too difficult, but expect from the intelligence of the officers, that they will be able, by taking closer advantage of the ground, by a more thorough preparation for the attack, and by the employment of suitable formations, to obtain in future the same results with inferior losses.
>
> (Signed) William.

The king was not advocating a loose order with all troops acting as skirmishers, but a more open formation with the company columns preceded by the skirmish line and using cover wherever possible to minimise casualties.

The Chassepot was an excellent weapon and the French quite justifiably placed great faith it. However, as with many developments in military hardware its strength lay in its use in defence, as amply demonstrated at the Battle of Gravelotte. For many of the combats in the war, it was the Germans doing the attacking and having to face the Chassepot over open ground. The German infantry did indeed learn the lesson and soon modified their tactics. At Le Bourget, a small village on the outskirts of Paris (and later the site of Paris's first airport), the Prussian Guard was again in action against French regulars and volunteers who had occupied the buildings. The Guard companies attacked in two platoons, with one giving covering fire while the other rushed forward seeking shelter who then gave fire in turn. During the long period of peace from the end of the war to the outbreak of the conflict beginning in 1914, the experience seemed to have been forgotten and the armies had to relearn the lessons of Gravelotte the hard way.

Prussian Cavalry

The mounted forces of the Prussian Army in July 1870 stood at two guard and eight line regiments of heavy cavalry, the cuirassiers; three guard and 16 line regiments of lancers, usually brigaded with the cuirassiers and classed as heavy; two guard and 19 regiments of medium cavalry, the dragoons; and one guard and 16 line regiments of light cavalry, the hussars. Added to this were two regiments of *cheveaulegers* (dragoons) from Hesse, four *reiter*, heavy cavalry regiments and two of lancers from Saxony, and a regiment of hussars from Brunswick. Bavaria provided two heavy cavalry regiments, cuirassiers and two of lancers together with six regiments of *cheveaulegers*. Also, from South Germany the Kingdom of Wurttemberg fielded four regiments of *reiters* (dragoons) and Baden three dragoon regiments. This mass of horsemen, 372 squadrons strong or 55,800 men, was distributed throughout the army with one regiment allocated to each infantry division and the rest organised into cavalry divisions.

Recruits for each regiment and squadron were taken from their district. The horses (like the men of the guard regiments) were drawn from the whole country, but categorisation of some sort was thought necessary, so they were classified by age in such a manner that in every squadron the age of each horse was indicated by the initial of its name. So, Paris, Priam and Perdita were (in 1872, for example) names of six-year-olds; Romulus, Reinette, and Robinson of seven-year-olds; while the rare initial Q (Quelle, Quaker, Quirinus) was reserved for horses of one-year volunteers, of whom there are seldom more than half-a-dozen in the same squadron (these examples were taken from the 9th Hussars).

The function of cavalry had changed over the years since Napoleon I and the Battle of Waterloo when Marshal Ney had led massed mounted attacks against British and allied infantry squares. In 1870 most cavalry leaders had grown up in this tradition and still saw the cavalry as the 'queen' of the battlefield, sweeping all before it in victorious charges. The French cavalry experience before 1870 had been chasing elusive Arab horsemen in Algeria and a few regimental actions against the Austrians in 1859 or watching British cavalry charging guns in the Crimea ('This is magnificent, but it is not war!'). Prussian cavalry history had been limited to a few skirmishes with the Danes in 1864 and one large sabre-against-sabre clash with Austrian horsemen in 1866. So, what to do with all this horse flesh and martial spirit? Part of the problem was that senior commanders had little idea of how to deploy and utilise their mounted asset. To put a man on a horse and prepare him for war was an expensive business and nobody wanted to risk wasting the investment. In 1866 cavalry had been kept in the rear of the armies, to be husbanded and released when the time was right. However, the time never seemed to be just right and when it was the cavalry were too far away from the action to be of any use.

Prussian dragoons skirmishing dismounted. (Watercolour by Maurice Toussaint)

Bavarian cuirassiers. (Watercolour by Maurice Toussaint)

The American Civil War had shown European observers, if they had cared to notice, how to use cavalry. Long-range reconnaissance in force, destroying enemy infrastructure, discovering valuable information and getting rifles in the right place quickly seemed to be the lessons. To a cavalryman the idea of 'mounted infantry' was anathema (even though this was the original purpose of dragoons in the 1600s, before some bright spark told them to use their swords instead of their muskets).

In 1866 senior officers were hampered by a lack of information about the enemy: where is he, what direction is he marching, how many men? This had been recognised at senior levels, but how to do it in the field? Some enterprising junior officers trained their squadrons in outpost duties and individual officers could lead a patrol behind enemy lines. The appearance, or even a rumour, of these small troops had caused the French to see '*Les Uhlans*' behind every tree and on every hilltop. Unfortunately, this potential had not been realised and there were times when Moltke had no idea where the French were and was unable to formulate a clear plan until contact had been re-established. The Prussians were not equipped to destroy French communications if they came across them. Illustrations show intrepid hussars cutting telegraph lines and railway tracks but looked at closely they only had their swords to do any damage. They were not issued with the tools to do the job properly – they needed axes, crowbars and explosives and pioneer equipment. The Austrians, not noted for innovation, had one enterprising senior officer who had already experimented with 'cavalry pioneers' equipped with tools to destroy enemy facilities, but just as importantly to repair, make bridges and improve their own army's communications. At the beginning of the war a Prussian cavalry patrol was sent to destroy a bridge and the officer in charge had the foresight to bring a section of sappers with their tools with him.

Another major drawback was the lack of proper armament: not all cavalry had modern firearms, as opposed to the French horsemen who were issued a carbine version of the excellent Chassepot rifle. The Dreyse carbine carried by medium and light cavalry had a limited range, about 200–300 paces, and with a reduced power cartridge and was therefore at a disadvantage when opposed to French infantry, or dismounted cavalry.

The heavy cavalry was not intended to be used for outpost work and their only firearm was a muzzle-loading percussion fire pistol and this was several years after the death of Samuel Colt in 1862 whose factory in the America had already produced 450,000 revolvers sold worldwide. This was very much a decision by the established military authorities, heavy cavalry was still regarded as the successors to the knights of old, where heavy horses carrying heavy riders would ride down enemy infantry and cavalry. And so, they reasoned, why did they need modern firearms?

Where German cavalry was used to gather information, they were at an immediate disadvantage when faced by a few hidden French riflemen. The remedy was to issue cavalrymen with captured French weapons, but the men were not trained in their use and the supply of ammunition could be a problem. However, an argument was used that if its purpose was to gather information, why did they need modern weapons? Where cavalry was used by the *Etappen* army to guard lines of communications they were at a similar disadvantage, well-armed *francs-tireurs* could easily fight off men armed only with swords or pistols. Later in the war cavalry patrols in difficult, wooded terrain were given infantry support, often carried in local transport, including farmer's carts.

The German authorities never really got to grips with the problem and by the 1890s all German cavalry had lances, but as a sop they also were issued with a carbine. It took trench warfare to finally dispel the 'cavalry' myth.

The cavalry really only came into its own at the Battle of Vionville-Mars La Tour where several squadrons charged the French in order to stop the Prussian infantry from being overwhelmed. But this was the only instance of a massed attack, with most cavalry actions during the war consisting of a single squadron or less. It also did not look good in the German order of battle, as the casualty list had been horrendous after the attack. Of the 800 cavalrymen who attacked the French gun lines barely half retuned. Among the wounded was Bismarck's son, Lieutenant Herbert von Bismarck.

Modern Technology

Two English pioneers – Sir William Cooke and his collaborator, Charles Wheatstone – invented a telegraph receiver/sender which used a dial with numbers and letters and had a pointer activated by an electric signal to spell out messages. However, problems with the electricity supply limited its use. In 1846 an impoverished Prussian army officer, Werner von Siemens, improved the mechanism and promoted his idea to the government. All that was needed was to undertake a test. There was a problem in that Prussians did not have a telegraph system at that time so there was nothing to test it on. Undaunted, Siemens and his engineer, Halske, won the contract to construct an electric telegraph line from Frankfurt to Berlin. Some 500 kms long it was completed in early 1849 thereby enabling messages to travel the distance in under an hour. The government took to the idea of the telegraph and soon lines were being erected all over Prussia and Germany. The rest of the world was not far behind.

Moltke could control the German forces in France from his office in Berlin by means of the telegraph, often more aware of the situation on the ground than his army commanders. As the German forces settled in a ring around Paris from mid-September, a new nerve centre was established at the Royal Headquarters at Versailles. An interesting painting by Anton von Werner shows Moltke and his staff approaching Paris, being cheered by columns of marching troops, with, off to one side, a section of telegraph troops, erecting poles and attaching cables.

The railway argument had been largely settled by 1870, with early critics dismissing railways as only good for movement of ammunition and supplies, and that marching regiments were much more adaptable than if they were tied to the lines of railway tracks. Moltke, however, was convinced of the superiority of rail transport and his views prevailed.

The Prussians were justly proud of their breech-loader, the first in the world to be issued as a universal weapon to troops. It had been developed by Nicholas Dreyse (the 'von' came later), who conceived of the idea of using a bolt to open and close the breech of his rifle, which was not so revolutionary really as he had started his working life as a lock maker in his father's factory. During the wars of Napoleon, he moved to Paris and worked with the Swiss gunmaker, Jean Pauly. The Pauly factory experimented with breech-loading and developed a cartridge with ball, powder and ignition enclosed together. Dreyse took the idea with him back to Germany where he tested several types of rifles, muzzle-loaders and later breech-loaders with this self-contained ammunition. His initial commercial enterprise was a factory making percussion caps, but he eventually gave that up to concentrate on his rifle. In the late 1820s he developed a muzzle-loading sporting rifle that fired his cartridge before coming up with the original bolt-action breech-loader.

In an inspired marketing ploy, he presented a sporting rifle using his system to the Prussian heir to the throne, Prince Wilhelm (the future German emperor), who was immediately aware of its potential. Overcoming his military advisors' conservatism, he ordered trials of the new weapon (the advisors were not enthusiastic as they had just adopted a new muzzle-loading rifle for the army). With Prince Wilhelm's support Dreyse's rifle was authorised for adoption by the Prussian Army as the 'Model 1841, Light Percussion Gun'. Early objections were overruled: if the needle was fragile, then carry spares which could be easily fitted; if it induced the soldiers to fire too quickly, so train them better in time of peace to conserve their fire.

The advantage is always given that the Prussian soldier could fire four or five shots per minute as against a muzzle-loader firing one or two, but the real advantage was in loading. The ease of placing a cartridge in the breech standing, kneeling or lying down meant that troops were always ready to fire – a fact that so unnerved Austrian soldiers in 1866 that their officers had difficulty getting them to stand up to reload as they were afraid of making themselves targets for the Prussians. The original iron barrels were rifled, giving them an advantage over smooth-bore weapons and in the 1850s cast steel barrels were used which meant finer tolerances in the bore could be achieved. The cartridge was consumed on firing which meant that no ejection method was required. Official reports stated that models issued in the 1840s were still in good condition in 1870. The advantage of rifling a gun barrel was that it imparted spin to the bullet greatly

Contemporary photograph of a Prussian Field Telegraph wagon.

The finer points of deploying telegraph cable in the field. (Drawing by Richard Knötel)

improving accuracy. The disadvantage was that the rifling grooves would become clogged with lead from the bullet or material generated by the combustion of the cartridge. Dreyse was aware of this and made his bullet slightly smaller than the bore of the barrel but encased it in a paper sabot that exactly fit the bore and picked up the requisite spin needed. The paper was burnt and ejected from the muzzle when the gun was fired.

A slightly improved model was introduced as the Model 62, which had a shorter barrel (84 cm as opposed to 90 cm of the earlier model) but no noticeable difference in performance. It was lighter and easier to manufacture and by 1870 about a third of the Prussian troops were carrying it, together with the Saxon, Baden and Hessian regiments. The Dreyse was produced in several different models, all using the same ammunition, thus simplifying the resupply problem. The cavalry carbine, however, had the same calibre, but used a lower power cartridge.

A shorter and lighter version of the Dreyse was introduced to the *jäger* battalions. It could be easily recognised by having a special rod bayonet fitted below the barrel which could be extended and locked in position by a spring catch in the nose cap. This Model 1854 was in service with the *jägers* until the introduction of an improved rifle, the Model 1865. The older model stayed in service and was converted to a pioneer rifle equipped with a sword bayonet with saw teeth on the back of the blade. The new model was easily recognisable as it had a double trigger within an enlarged trigger guard. The purpose of the leading trigger was to set the amount of pressure needed to fire the rifle with a gentle touch on the second trigger, so improving aiming. It could be fitted with a sword bayonet.

Comparing the performance of the Dreyse with the known capabilities of the Chassepot the German authorities decided that an improvement was necessary. The shape and weight of the bullet was altered, and an improved bolt head fitted. Unkind critics have called this a direct copy of the Chassepot bolt head. A few thousand rifles were thus altered, enough to equip three regiments, before the war broke out. This was called the 'Beck' conversion, after its designer, and could be recognised by a small screw head fitted just forward of the bolt handle.

Wall, or rampart guns had been part of the armoury almost since the invention of firearms. Dreyse developed his bolt action for a weapon to be used with a support, and an early version had been used by the Prussians during the siege of Duppel in Denmark in 1864, where they had a metal frame resting against the wall of the trenches. The gun used in 1870, especially in siege operations, had a steel tube stock with a large shoulder rest. It fired a steel bullet (as opposed to the lead bullet of standard rifles) of 23.5-inch calibre, thus giving it longer range and greater hitting power.

Dreyse designed a pistol version of his rifle mechanism to replace the muzzle-loading cavalry percussion weapon. It used the same bolt action to open the breech for loading which required the horseman to use both hands. The ammunition was the same as the cavalry carbine. About 200 pistols were made in 1856 for field testing; however, they were not accepted and the carbine for cavalry was adopted instead. In a similar manner, the excellent Bavarian Werder rifle was also the basis for a handgun. However, like the Dreyse pistol, this one-shot weapon also needed two hands to load.

The Bavarians also came up with a '*Mitrailleuse*' volley gun of their own. A battery of four guns accompanied each Bavarian army corps into France. It was named the 'Feldl' gun after its inventor and had four barrels and fired the Werder metallic cartridge. There was a trigger crank on the left side. The first two models weighed, respectively, 367 kg (with a supply of 720 cartridges) and 250 kg (with a provision of 400 cartridges); the third weighed only 80 kg (with 750 cartridges). The sights could be set from 200 to 2,000 paces, about 1,500 metres, with a rate of fire of 300 rounds per minute. The ammunition was supplied by eight magazines of 41 cartridges each and was gravity fed. The loading mechanism had, according to the manual, only four parts: a propeller drum, which operated two bolts fitted with firing pins, and a carrier which distributed the cartridges alternately in front of each bolt. Movement was given to the whole system by a lever to which a reciprocating movement was applied from top to bottom and from bottom to top. A crew of six men was required to load each magazine by hand, to keep the gun in action.

The lightness of the gun was due to its having only the four barrels and the wheeled carriage was made of thin iron strips, similar to that used on farm machinery. The gun and limber were pulled by a four-horse team, the limber holding 6,864 cartridges, the magazines, and tools. The guns had two ammunition limbers (captured from the French at the Battle of Woerth) each containing over 16,000 cartridges. Feldl was asked to inspect the guns in reserve near Paris in December 1870 and found them badly maintained with the magazines deformed because of the use of thin sheet metal. He undertook some repairs, but the Bavarian Army decided that they were unreliable and withdrew them from service. The large box below the centre of the axel was to collect the spent cartridge cases which were sent back to the factory for reloading.

The French Chassepot rifle was captured in vast numbers, along with its ammunition. The Germans were well aware of its superiority and used many of them to equip some light cavalry squadrons who were at a disadvantage when confronting French infantry and cavalry while scouting ahead of their main bodies. The Chassepot was also issued in limited numbers to the front-line trenches around Paris, where the troops were also at a disadvantage against their Chassepot-armed opposite numbers.

Minor Tactics

Battlefield tactics were laid down in regulations and by and large followed in the field, although some senior officers had to be reminded about the use of skirmishers followed at prescribed intervals by company columns with artillery support. In the many small actions throughout the zone between occupied France and French-controlled territory, officers, mainly middle-ranking company and battalion commanders, local initiative was allowed.

German generals also adapted to local situations: on the day of the Battle of Bapaume, 3 January 1871, General von Bentheim on the River Seine faced a large French force coming from Le Havre. The French had for same days been building up their forces on the left bank of the river, threatening the city of Rouen. At 5 o'clock, while it was till dark, the Germans launched an attack on the French troops who were still in their quarters. After a brisk fight the French fell back, leaving behind several hundred prisoners (between 300 and 500), four standards and two guns. To pursue the enemy, Bentheim sent two squadrons of cavalry, two pieces of horse artillery and a company of infantry carried in wagons to keep up. The result of the action was many more prisoners and two further guns taken. But what is one to do if you are outnumbered and out gunned? A small German cavalry force, from a regiment of lancers, was faced by a French reconnaissance consisting of two infantry battalions and a regiment of cavalry. The lancers dismounted, took cover in a small hamlet and waited until the French infantry had advanced to within 1,000 metres when they opened fire with their pistols (the only firearms carried by the lancers). Needless to say, the range of the Prussian cavalry pistol was less than 100 metres, but they could and did generate a fair amount of smoke and noise which they kept up until the advancing French became convinced that the hamlet was occupied by a large body of infantry, who then made a hasty retreat.

German 'Brutality'

Stories soon circulated about the way that French civilians were treated by the invading forces. This made for good propaganda for the French newspapers, but it could not always be verified by an independent enquirer.

Mr Henry Sutherland Edwards, one of the correspondents for *The Times*, did take the trouble to find out the truth of a much-publicised reported incident:

> I was told many stories at Nancy of the brutality of the German soldiery, and was actually

Prussian Landwehr.

> introduced to a young lady whom, it was said, a Bavarian had struck with the butt end of his musket because she had given a brioche (charmingly appropriate food!) to a wounded officer. But the blow turned out to have been a push given in a crowd, and the young lady admitted that on her slapping the Bavarian on the face, the man, instead of killing her, as in her fright at what she had so rashly done she had fully expected, only burst out laughing; so that he was not such a very brutal person after all.

The Occupation

One innkeeper reported to Sutherland Edwards that the enemy had taken all the livestock they could find.

> He could give me no milk, because there were no longer any cows. He would be unable to plough his land, because he had no horses. There was not a horse in the village, so that there could be no ploughing, no sowing, no harvest next year; nothing but famine. As for the bits of paper given in acknowledgment of the things taken – the "requisitions", as they were called – he looked upon them as worthless. At all events, no money could be raised upon them; and numbers of poor people would be ruined before the time of redemption arrived. He considered that it would have

Bavarian troops entering Paris, note the pioneers at the head of the column, followed by the band. (*Illustrated London News*)

Bavarian soldiers in the Tuileries. (*The Graphic*)

An interesting study of Prussian sailors at Versailles. (*Illustrated London News*)

> been better policy on the part of the French not to have allowed the Prussians to come into France at all. He, for his part, had done his best to prevent them, not personally, but through a substitute, whom he had bought to replace his son, now a tradesman in Paris. The substitute, who had cost him 2,400 francs, had performed wonders on the field of battle, and at Forbach (part of the Battle of Spicheren) had been badly wounded.

As the troops advanced, they outpaced their commissariat and had to use whatever was available locally. The Prussians had strict rules against looting, but whatever name was given to it, such as 'requisitioning', it amounted to much the same thing. When some locals had the temerity to complain, the German officers felt bound to take action (not just out of pity, but an army depending on looting soon loses its respect for discipline and becomes a rabble). The landlady of an inn remonstrated that 'they have stolen my linen, my handkerchiefs, and, worst of all, my wedding shawl'. She added, however, that the colonel commanding the regiment to which the culprits belonged had done his best to discover them, and had told her that if she could point them out he would punish them severely and make them restore as much as possible of what they had stolen. But one soldier, she continued, is so much like another, and there were so many soldiers quartered every day in the same house, that to identify the offenders was impossible.

The threat of disruption caused by *francs-tireurs*, whether real or imagined, had an impact on the German operations. During the siege of Belfort by General von Werder, the Germans became acutely concerned for their lines of communication. The remedy was to mount a specific operation against the *francs-tireurs*. A small 'army' was organised of all arms, four battalions of infantry, three from the 5th Baden Infantry Regiment and one from the 6th. Eight squadrons of cavalry, three artillery batteries and a pioneer company made up the force. This detachment did succeed in breaking up some French *franc-tireur* companies, but not in the numbers they hoped. It seems that the strength of the bands of volunteers had been greatly exaggerated. Nevertheless, the mere rumour and later the presence of small bands of volunteers had had the desired effect from the French point of view of raising morale among the local population and distracting numbers of German troops from more pressing duties.

The Polish Problem

In the Prussian province of Posen (now Poznan, formerly part of Napoleon's Duchy of Warsaw and administered by Prussia after the Congress of Vienna in 1815), with its large Polish population, there was much sympathy for the French and angry demonstrations at the news of Prussian victories which generated an outburst of Polish national feeling. Calls were made for Polish recruits to desert from the Prussian Army, though with little success. A report on the situation, sent to Bismarck on 16 August 1870, led to the sending of reserve troops to occupy the province and overawe the populace. The war became a significant event in German–Polish relations. The Prussian government began a campaign of Germanisation, restricting use of the Polish language and customs and imposing German officials in local institutions.

Polish recruits in the army were gathered in district regiments, similar to the rest of the German regular and *Landwehr* forces. Many Polish reservists had little idea who the French actually were: one description, admittedly in a novel, has two Polish privates explaining to one another, 'of the three nations known …, living in the centre were the Poles; on the one side were the Russians, on the other the Germans. But there were various kinds of Germans, so the French must be like the Germans, only worse.[6] With that our heroes boarded the train to take them to Steinmetz's First Army on the River Saar.'

---

6 Taken from an 1882 story "Bartek Zwycięzca" ("Bartek the Conqueror") by Polish writer Henryk Sienkiewicz, best known for his Ancient Roman period novel *Quo Vadis*.

Demobilisation

What happened when the troops, for several months enduring the hardships of campaign, were sent home after peace was declared. For the *Landwehr*, not being regular soldiers, it meant handing back their trappings of war. On reaching their hometown, first the rifles and side arms were given up; the following day it was the remaining cartridges, packs and uniform clothes. The men then appeared in their civilian dress which had been kept at the depot. A Guard *Landwehr* officer reported that his company now looked like farmers in their long smocks, or workmen in blouses or the fine outfit of a well to do citizen. The last duty of the *Landwehr* men was to form a square about the officers who stood in the centre. 'Farewell men of the Guard *Landwehr*,' calls the commanding officer, 'A good soldier will also be a good citizen. Fare you well! You are dismissed to your homes.' Even after active service each man was expected to continue to do his duty in civilian life.

The War in German Art

Depictions of battles, soldiers and incidents of the war appeared in German illustrated newspapers from the outbreak of hostilities. At the 25th anniversary of the war a huge number of books were published, many in the 'illustrated' or 'popular' style. Artists continued to use themes of the 1870–1871 period right up until the First World War.

Georg Bleibtreu accompanied the Prussian Army in the field during the Danish War of 1864 and the Austrian War of 1866 and was attached to the Prussian Crown Prince's staff in 1870. He painted many monumental canvases, with one of the fighting at Duppel purchased by the king of Prussia.

Louis Braun was a south German who followed the Austrian Army in the 1864 Danish war, and later followed the German troops in 1870. His panorama painting of the Battle of Sedan was exhibited in several venues in Germany.

Ludwig Berger was well known for his large decorative paintings, but he illustrated many books on military subjects, particularly the 1870–1871 campaign.

Appointed an official war artist in 1870, Wilhelm Camphausen had seen action in Denmark in 1864 and in the field in 1866 and specialised in book illustration and portraits of German princes and generals.

Feodor Dietz first exhibited at the Paris Salon in 1838. He became painter to the court of Baden in 1839. He painted military portraits, notably Ernest II of Saxe-Coburg-Gotha (Queen Victoria's brother-in-law) leading his troops at the Battle of Eckernforde in Schleswig in 1849. In 1862 he was appointed professor at the academy in Karlsruhe, but at the outbreak of the Franco–Prussian War he gave up his post to join the volunteer ambulance services. He died at Gray in eastern France during the campaign.

Later German artists drew on the war for their inspiration, usually on commission from participants in the war and from regimental messes. Carl Rochling and Richard Knoetel both painted large battle-themed canvases and provided illustrations for children's and adult books and newspapers. Knoetel's studies of uniforms brought him into contact with similar enthusiasts across Europe and between 1890 and 1914 he published his '*Uniformkunde*' series, a thousand coloured plates each with a commentary. His son continued the series in the 1920s and 1930s.

Women in Germany

In 1868 Lina Morgenstern established a School for Further Education of Young Ladies and in the following year the Berlin Society for Child Protection, which sought to combat the high mortality rate among babies born out of wedlock, as well as the Association for the Education of Women Workers, together with the feminist Louise Otto Pelers. When the war broke out in 1870, '*Suppenlina*', as she was now nicknamed, organised the care of soldiers passing through Berlin. In only 12 days, she and her colleagues cared for

59,000 men, providing them with food, a pharmacy, a photographic studio, and a field postal service to enable them to write to their families. Her work brought her to the attention of Kaiser Wilhelm and his wife, the Empress Augusta, who visited her headquarters. The latter became a dedicated supporter of Lina Morgenstern's work, donating large sums of money and enlisting further gifts from others, while also serving as patron of the Berlin Association of People's Kitchens. Discovering that medical aid was inadequately provided for, Lina Morgenstern hired two doctors and amassed supplies of bandages, blankets and hot meals. Only after she had appealed to the empress were army doctors sent in.

The Cross of Merit for Women and Maidens and the War Commemorative Medal for 1870/71 for Non-combatants

The design of the award gives proof of its high standing. It was mainly awarded to noblewomen for their work in raising money and facilities for the wounded. The medal is similar to the Iron Cross, with the exception of the emblem of the Red Cross in the centre of the obverse. The reverse holds the royal crown above the intertwined monograms 'A' and 'W' (for Empress Augusta and Emperor Wilhelm) and the date of 1870 over 1871. The cross measured 33.4 mm wide and 33.3 mm high with a 35 mm wide ribbon. The cross was worn suspended from a bow on the left side. The ribbon is the same as that of the Iron Cross for non-combatants: white with black edges. The Commemorative War Medal for Non-combatants has the white ribbon edged black with a red centre stripe.

Chapter 4

Medical Services

French Medical Organisation

An American volunteer surgeon serving with the French army noted in his diary, that:

> The medical appointments of each regiment consisted of a regimental surgeon, a surgeon-major, two assistants and four *infirmiers* to each battalion. The combined medical staff of a division of two brigades formed the ambulance corps of that respective division. It was with these division ambulances that new officers and men were to be incorporated without being detailed to any particular regiment. The Convention of Geneva had established depots in all the principal cities and towns of Europe. Shortly after the declaration of war against Prussia, materials, such as clothing, bedding, lint, medicines, surgical appliances, etc., were poured by patriotic subjects into the French depots.

However, his direct observation of the French medical services in action was far from complimentary. Lack of organisation seemed to be the word of the day, this was not even the famous *Système D* in operation, but utter confusion at best and criminality at worst. The sheer magnitude of coping with the vast numbers of wounded simply overwhelmed what organisation was attempted to be set up. The fact that the French, after the frontier battles, were always moving back, meant that any facilities that were organised were immediately left behind as the troops retreated. This also happened on the battles on the Loire and the districts in the north where Faidherbe lost ground to the Prussians.

For all the French experience in war, in Crimea and Italy, little preparation had been put in place for the outbreak of the war in 1870. The numbers of wounded who were picked up from the battlefield, who died on the way, or in first aid posts or in hospitals was horrific. Of course, the 'germ theory' of infection was not then understood and 'hospital fever' was often cited as a cause of death (typhus or gangrene prevalent due to poor sanitation). The American hospital which was constructed from wood and canvas and set up in the open was far healthier than the enclosed buildings used by the French, or as many of the German facilities were for that matter. The American medical volunteers had learned much from their experiences during the Civil War, including the fact that good ventilation, cleanliness and dedicated nursing were important in saving lives.

The French used a special saddle with a seat which fitted on either side of a mule and could therefore bring two wounded from the battlefield to be treated. Observers have commented that this method was extremely uncomfortable and gave the patients extra torment. The French hospital wagons only had straw spread out on the floorboards, which again was uncomfortable. Peasants' carts pressed into service were no better.

French medical troops in the field. (Drawing by Eduard Detaille)

Transporting wounded by river steamers, on the Canal de la Marne, to Paris ambulances. (*The Graphic*)

Parisian schoolboys collecting gifts for the relief of the wounded. (*Illustrated London News*)

The Organisation of the Prussian Medical Column

A sanitary column, or detachment, comprised six two-horse ambulance carriages for the conveyance of the severely wounded; 42 bearers, or stretchers, for the carriage, by hand, of injured men from point to point, to or from the ambulance-carriages to the bandage-places, or initial first aid posts, or to the field hospitals; three wheeled-supports for stretchers; two two-horse wagons, specially constructed for dispensary purposes and equipped with instruments, surgical dressings, materials, splints, chloroform, medicines and medical comforts. These 'medical comforts' consisted of, to each ambulance detachment, the quantities being equally divided between the two sanitary wagons: English biscuits, 10 lbs [4.5 kg]; brandy, six bottles; chocolate in small tablets to be eaten, 6 lbs [2.7 kg]; Liebig's Extract of Meat, in 1 lb [0.45 kg] pots, 6 lbs [2.7 kg]; roasted coffee, 10 lbs [4.5 kg]; white and red wine, nine dozen bottles; vinegar, eight bottles; lemon juice, 1 lb [0.45 kg]; and sugar, 4 lbs [1.8 kg].

There followed two wagons each pulled by two horses for stores and baggage; two staff-surgeons, first- and second-class mounted; five assistant-surgeons mounted; one field-apothecary, or dispenser mounted; two chief, or upper hospital helpers; six hospital helpers; eight military sick attendants; one second-class cavalry captain mounted; two lieutenants, first and second, mounted; one paymaster, or treasurer, mounted; one head, or chief, non-commissioned officer; four sergeants; eight corporals; 12 lance-corporals bearers; 20 privates as bearers; four buglers; three mounted Train [that is, Transport] non-commissioned officers; three Train corporals, mounted; 23 trained soldiers; 11 drivers and 12 grooms; 41 horses, 19 saddle and 22 harness. A number of wagons, or country carts, well filled with straw, were added when the ambulance detachment was likely to be brought up to action; and at other times country carts, carrying forage, provisions and so on accompanied the detachment.

A Prussian chaplain acting as stretcher bearer in the field. (Drawing by Carl Becker)

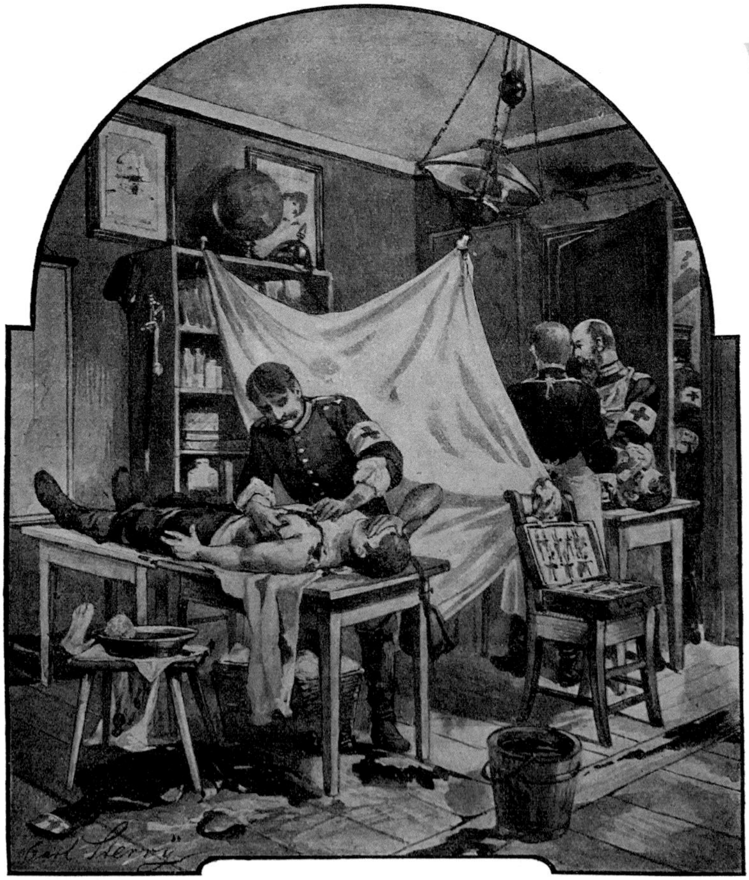

A temporary German field hospital in a school house.

The line of march was ordered beginning with a small party of bearers, then the captain, the medical officers, the lieutenants and the paymaster, all mounted. The company of stretcher bearers came next and were immediately followed by the ambulance carriages for the conveyance of wounded. The sanitary, or medicine wagons, and the stores, or baggage wagons, then follow, and at the rear were country wagons, or peasants' carts with forage and provisions, and the remount horses for the surgeons and assistant-surgeons.

These ambulance detachments are intended for dressing, or first aid stations, and the collection and removal of the wounded from the battlefield. In minor engagements they were not employed; the wounded in such small encounters, as already mentioned, being attended to by the regimental surgeons, assisted in the rear by the medical officers of troops not actually engaged. The ambulance carriages were not used to carry the sick on the line of march, or of sick in camp; nor were they intended to meet the necessities of distant removals of wounded. They were not intended for use in the evacuation of sick or wounded. In general actions, or important battles, the ambulance detachments were put into operation. That attached to each infantry division accompanied the troops directly into action on the battlefield. The orders for its movement and application were received direct from the division commander, who also arranged, according to circumstances, whether the whole, or one section, should come into play, or whether the two sections should act independently, on account of the extension of the line of battle. These sections may be ordered to establish separate 'troop bandage-places', or they may have to join in the formation of the first aid places. In default of such orders, and when there is risk in delay, these arrangements are to be made by the division-surgeon. If from unexpected change in military operations, or other unforeseen circumstances, such instructions become inapplicable, the officer commanding the ambulance detachment took command and gave the appropriate orders.

Stretcher bearer of a Prussian ambulance unit.

In arranging the first aid posts, any buildings in the area were used; if none existed, an operating tent was pitched in a suitable situation hopefully under cover from enemy fire. The first aid post was distinguished by a national ensign (Prussian, Bavarian, or the German state), and by the red cross flag of the Geneva Convention and at night by a red lantern. The ambulance vehicles were to be pushed forward as far as possible, even if it meant coming under small arms fire. The surgeons attached to the ambulance detachments, with a proportion of the regimental medical officers, manned these forward aid posts. The two wagons containing instruments, surgical dressings and chloroform were also stationed close to the first aid posts.

Walking wounded and such injured men as could be helped or carried away during the action received attention as they needed, and then they were removed back to the field hospitals. As soon as the fighting ceased, the real business of collecting, attending to and removing the fallen was carried out. This was done under the orders of the commanding officer by the company of trained bearers belonging to the ambulance detachments. Of course, this assumes that the Germans were masters of the battlefield and had been victorious in the action. As this was not always the case, the fate of the wounded was left to chance or the good will of the enemy if they had won the day.

Four men were allotted to each stretcher: two to carry the wounded man on the stretcher, and two as reliefs, and to pick up the arms, kit and effects of the casualty. The company of bearers belonging to the ambulance detachment was divided into two wings, each under the immediate orders of an officer. Each wing was subdivided into sections of 12 men, with three stretchers, under the orders of an NCO. These squads of bearers were to regularly patrol the battlefield and its vicinity. They were to examine carefully the whole of the fallen, separating the living from the dead, giving help to the former and removing them to the nearest first aid post, to the ambulance carriages, or perhaps to the field hospitals, if these happen to occupy advance positions. This again depended on who controlled the battlefield after the fighting had ceased.

This separation of the living from the dead required great care and attention, as not unfrequently a man who was not mortally injured may, from loss of blood, collapse, previous over-fatigue or other temporary cause be in a state almost resembling death. Therefore, every 'dead' man had to be examined to ascertain if the injury he had received was mortal.

The patrols of bearers also had to collect and take charge of stray arms, accoutrements and other articles of value. When they had collected and removed all the wounded found in the open, they systematically searched the woods, ditches and adjacent areas in which combat may have been engaged or to which wounded men may have crawled for protection or shelter. The severely wounded were placed on stretchers which were either carried by the bearers or travelled on wheel-supports. These wheeled stretchers were on many occasions found to be extremely useful and afforded many special advantages. In some instances,

Dispatching packages from the Prussian embassy for the German sick and wounded. (*Illustrated London News*)

say in crossing fields traversed by ditches or deep ruts, they had to be raised and lifted across; but this was found to be as easily effected as with the ordinary stretcher, and harm is much less likely to occur to the injured man from the bearers stumbling, as was liable to happen with the ordinary stretcher, when the bearers suddenly come upon a ditch. Moreover, considerably fewer bearers could convey a larger number of wounded over longer distances using these wheeled stretchers.

At the main aid post the directing surgeon makes a judicious distribution of the duties and of the members of the staff. In general, the medical officers were separated into three divisions, each of which was distinct in situation, succeeding each other in duties and in professional function. The first division specially attended to the mortally wounded and to the slightly injured. All who arrive at the station have their garments cut off, the blood and dust removed, and are submitted to a regular examination, provided this has not been previously done on the field, as shown by a card attached to the injured man. The slightly wounded, superficial and flesh injuries, after the necessary surgical manipulations and having been dressed, are sent further back to field hospitals. The mortally injured, to whom further removal would only augment the pains of dying, are placed aside in a sheltered spot, and such relief as their cases permit is afforded. It was very necessary, however, to carefully re-examine these cases subsequently, as it was sometimes found that even seriously wounded men sometimes recovered, although at the time they are first brought in from the battlefield they appeared to be dying, and no hope is at the time entertained of saving them.

The second division applied difficult and complicated bandages, surgical appliances requiring time for their proper adjustment, plaster of Paris, or splints. Cases of injury requiring the above, and instances of grave bone injury, where immediate amputation did not appear to be indicated, are treated here. Fractures of the lower extremity, especially of the thigh, belong to this category.

The third division undertook those capital operations that must absolutely be performed without delay even at the bandage places. To this category belong ligature of the main arteries, on account of bleeding; tracheotomy, for injuries of the larynx and windpipe; and, above all, amputation of the larger limbs, on account of complete destruction or tearing off by heavy shot or shell. In this period, medical aid was relatively simple, flesh wounds were treated with compresses and bandages with the intention of slowing the flow of blood. Where bullets or shell fragments had caused broken bones in the arms or legs, amputation was the only real course of action. Without surgery the patient would certainly die and quick removal of the damaged limb might just save his life.

After the first careful examination of the injury, and on the termination of the necessary surgical manipulation, the medical officer is obliged to fasten to the man's clothes a 'diagnosis tablet'. On this card it was specified, the grade or degree of the man's fitness to be transported. Furthermore, it stated briefly and clearly the description of the injury, the transit, attention and care. These labels, where properly filled up, were of great utility in preventing frequent and repeated examinations and dressing of an injured man by successive surgeons, into whose hands he may pass, and facilitated the regular distribution of the wounded in directions suitable to their injuries.

Each army corps had 12 field hospitals: four for each infantry division, and four available for general duty with either or both divisions, or for detached purposes. The field hospitals followed the advancing army corps as closely as circumstances permitted, their movements and position regulated by the instructions of the principal medical officer under orders from the general commanding. The details of movement were arranged by the field hospital director, each field hospital being under the sole management and authority of the medical officer in charge, as far as internal organisation is concerned. A field hospital was calculated for the accommodation of 200 patients as a minimum; but it was considered capable of extension to a much larger number. The field hospitals were not attached to the 'Train' but belonged to the 'administration' of the army corps.

During the campaign, consulting surgeons, with the rank of a surgeon-general, were added to the army. After a battle the consulting surgeons worked at the field hospitals, giving advice and assistance on the spot; but they were more generally engaged in the hospitals. They went the rounds of the medical

Railway wagons used as hospitals. (*Illustrated London News*)

Section drawing of a carriage on a German hospital train.

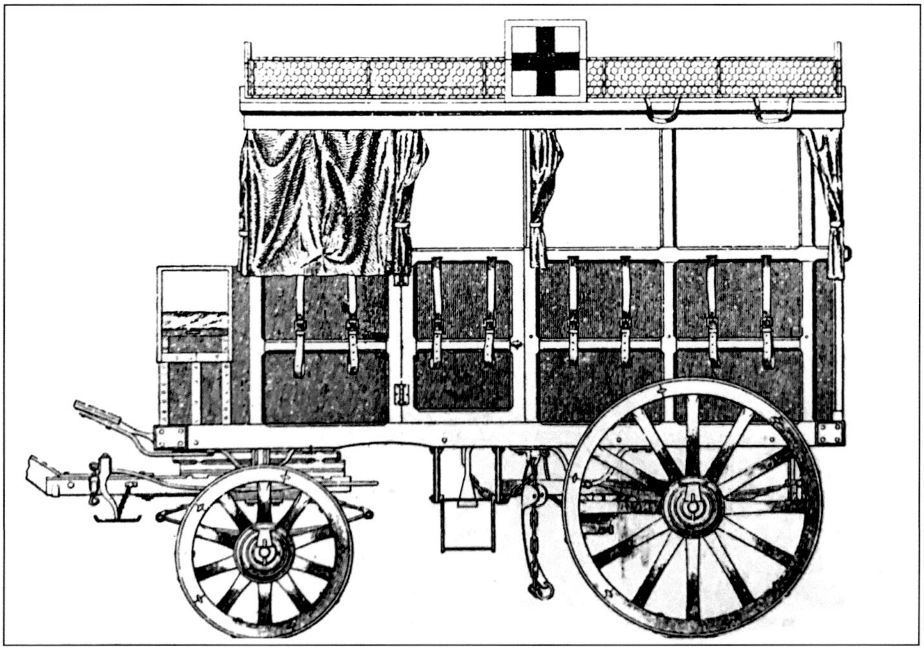

Bavarian hospital transport wagon.

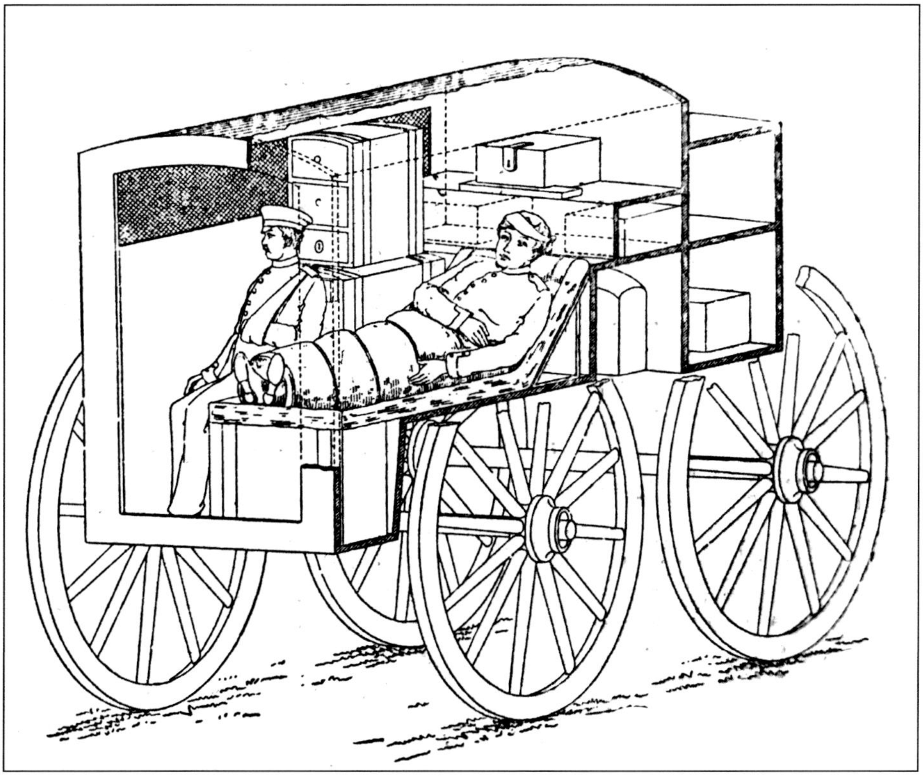

Schematic drawing of a Saxon hospital wagon.

establishments in their district as often as possible, timing their visits as far as practicable according to the hours of the regular visits of the military surgeons. In these inspections the chief surgeon of the hospital mentioned any difficulties and decided with the consulting surgeon the proper means of remedy. The latter was required to mention everything that occurs to him about the treatment of the sick in general, and anything of importance. If there was a difference of opinion, due attention was paid to the judgment of the consulting surgeon. In such circumstances, if he found the further value of his prescriptions opposed by orders, he gave his directions in writing, and these had to be implicitly followed. The responsibility of such directions rested with the consulting surgeon, who made known the circumstances to the military medical superiors.

This description of the Prussian medical column is based on official regulations and relates to procedures to be adopted in most conditions. However, once battle had been joined the conditions were far from ideal and the treatment of the wounded often fell short of what the military medical professionals had decreed. The regulations were based on the best of intentions as devised by a special committee convened in Berlin after the war against Austria and her allies in 1866.

The Bandage of Doctor Esmarch

Doctor Johannes Friedrich August (later 'von') Esmarch had served in the Schleswig-Holstein Army in the war against the Danes in 1848–1850 first as a junior surgeon and later upon promotion as senior surgeon in a field hospital. After the war he became the director of a hospital and was appointed professor at the university in Kiel. In 1864 he was again in the field during the Second Schleswig-Holstein War. In 1866 he was summoned to Berlin as a member of the hospital commission and superintendent of the surgical departments of the city's hospitals. In 1870 he was appointed surgeon-general to the Prussian Army and chief consulting surgeon in Berlin.

In the 1830s a Swiss doctor had advocated the use of a universal bandage to be carried for use in first aid to hold a dressing in place or support a limb and Esmarch realised that this could be a great help to the wounded if used on the battlefield. He saw that quick action was needed if lives and limbs were to be saved. He devised a bandage that cut the Swiss original in half diagonally which resulted in a triangular piece of linen or cotton, the base measuring 4 feet and the sides 2 feet 10 inches (122 cm x 86 cm). It could be used folded or open and was capable of being applied in 32 different ways.

The first version was printed with illustrations of how the bandage could be used, with each application given a number. However, it was thought the depiction of wounded soldiers was rather too graphic and the second version had just plain figures showing the bandage in use. All Prussian soldiers were issued with this bandage as part of their kit.

One of the uses of the bandage was as a tourniquet to halt the flow of blood from a wound and the modern Esmarch bandage is still in use today, now in the form of a strip, up to 10 cm wide, of elasticated material taken from a long or pre-cut roll.

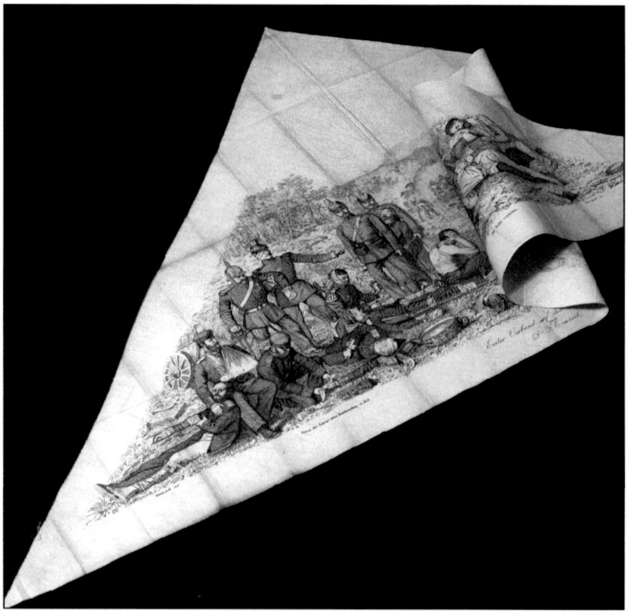

The original Esmarch triangular bandage.

Medical Volunteers

Clara Barton

American nurse Clara Barton.

Many volunteers arrived in France and Prussia during the conflict, spurred by sympathy for the wounded and offering their assistance to the authorities of either side. As the military medical services were overwhelmed, their help was greatly appreciated. The volunteer medical helpers, in the main, consisted of individual doctors and surgeons who would be instantly useful (although put on probation in the Prussian service) and amateurs with some medical knowledge who could be put to work in hospitals after the surgeons had done their often-gruesome tasks.

Among the latter was an American visitor who had come to Europe before the war to regain her strength after a period of intensive work. That work was caring for wounded and sick soldiers during the American Civil War. At that time the United States had no organised Red Cross Association and Clara Barton had undertaken her mission of mercy with little help. She had also acted as a link between soldiers and their families, trying to find the whereabouts of men missing in action to inform family and friends. From this she realised that medical care was only part of the solution and that supplying food and clothes and giving hope were just as important.

Clara Barton was supervised in her work by the International Red Cross and the German Red Cross where she met Louise, the Grand Duchess of Baden, who was the daughter of King Wilhelm of Prussia. The grand duchess encouraged women to work as volunteer nursing assistants and she also supported the establishment of schools of nursing. This chimed in with Clara Barton's views that more should be done for war casualties than just applying a bandage. The grand duchess also issued Barton with a Red Cross badge and more importantly a railway pass to Strasbourg. The city had been besieged by the Germans early in the war and was badly damaged by artillery shells.

On arrival at Strasbourg, Barton found thousands of citizens cold, hungry and without hope. As well as the devastations of war, sickness was also rife: typhoid, caused by drinking contaminated water, and smallpox was raging throughout France and spreading across Europe. Barton had to struggle with the language as she did not speak any French or the Alsatian dialect spoken in Strasbourg. Initially, she helped in a soup kitchen, but soon realised that more was needed. She explained to the grand duchess that just giving food handouts would only make beggars of the people, and hit upon the idea of organising sewing establishments for the women of the city who would be paid for their work, clothing first the citizens and then the people in the local villages, who in turn would exchange the clothing for food. This was the start of rejuvenating the local economy. So well did the work of Barton become known that the now German emperor, Wilhelm, awarded her the special Iron Cross adorned with a small enamel Red Cross emblem in the centre of the arms. This cross still exists and is hung from a black-edged white ribbon, which is normally reserved for military recipients. The medal is also displayed with a civilian ribbon in reversed colours. Clara Barton continued her efforts on behalf of the Red Cross on her return to the United States and through her diligence the American Red Cross came into being.

Coralie Cahen

Coralie Cahen, French volunteer nurse.

Coralie Cahen was 43, the widow of a doctor, when the war broke out in the summer of 1870. According to her own account, she was asked to aid the wounded in Metz. Using equipment of the French Red Cross organisation, the *Société de secours aux blessés militaire*, she organised the retrieval of wounded soldiers from the battlefields and, with the help of other Metz ladies, set up a large hospital to care for them. The service catered for NCOs and ordinary soldiers (officers had their own service). In 1871 she visited 66 Prussian prisons where captured French soldiers were being held and pleaded personally with Empress Augusta of Germany for their release. In 1872, when the German government was proving awkward and failing to cooperate on this issue, Cahen discovered 59,000 files on the prisoners in Berlin and succeeded in getting the information transferred to Paris. This was the first news available in France on many of those who had been captured. In 1888 Cahen was awarded the Legion of Honour for her war work.

The English Ambulance

A prominent British resident of Paris, Richard Wallace, contributed funds for the establishment of two ambulances during the siege: one for French wounded and one for 'sick and destitute' British citizens. He also contributed more than £12,000 of funding for the ambulances as part of the 2.5 million francs he gave to relieve suffering in Paris during the war. Despite having the opportunity to get out of Paris, Wallace chose to remain in the city throughout the war. The hospitals, staffed by English surgeons, became known as the '*Ambulance Anglaise*' ('English Ambulance'), though Wallace named the mobile first aid wagons of the unit after his father, the Marquess of Hertford. The unit provided a hospital of 50 beds in the city and absorbed some of the staff of the American Ambulance after it was disbanded in March.

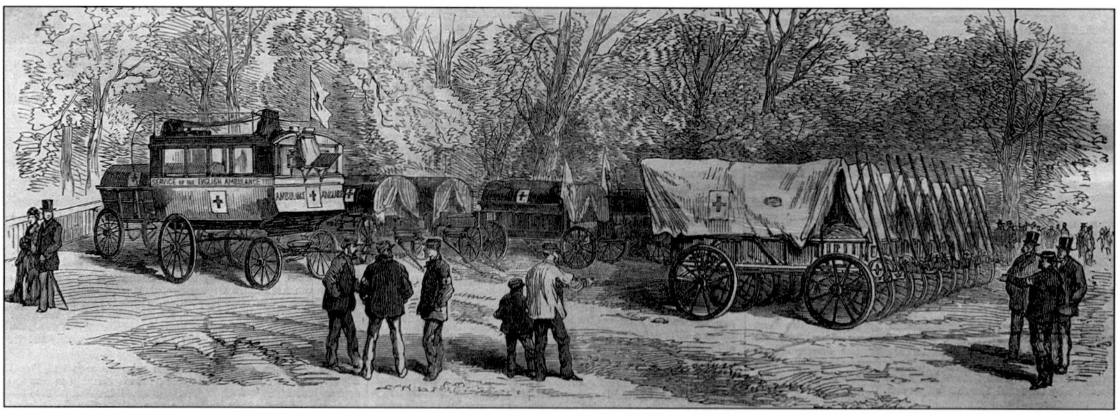

English ambulance train encamped outside the park of St Germains, Paris. (*Illustrated London News*)

After the war, Wallace's ambulances were taken into the Hertford British Hospital, established in Paris by Wallace on 15 October 1871. As a result of his work, he was said to be the most popular British resident of the city. He was honoured by having a street named for him and received the Legion of Honour from France and a baronetcy from Queen Victoria. His house at Manchester Square, in London, now houses his family collection of art and armour, known as the Wallace Collection.

The Anglo-American Ambulance

The Anglo-American Ambulance was led by Confederate American Civil War veteran, J. Marion Sims, who was then resident in France, and British surgeon William MacCormac. The new ambulance was partially funded by the British Society for Aid to the Sick and Wounded in War and consisted of eight American and a similar number of English medical staff with three ambulance wagons. All but one of the Americans were former Confederate Army surgeons. After the defeat of the French imperial armies, the ambulance was re-united at Sedan under Prussian occupation and erected 36 tents to accommodate the large number of wounded from the recent battles and those given to their care by the Prussian forces. The ambulance was granted permission to leave Sedan for Paris on 4 October and travelled via Belgium and Rouen. However, it proved impossible to enter the capital due to the ongoing siege, so the unit was placed at the disposal of the Prussian Army at Versailles by Robert Loyd-Lindsay of the British National Society for Aid to the Sick and Wounded in War. At around this time the ambulance changed its previously French-inspired uniform for that of the British Army's Royal Artillery undress uniform.

Private and public carriages used for the ambulance service outside Paris. (*Illustrated London News*)

British Red Cross Society

John Furley met with Robert Loyd-Lindsay to ask him if he would help set up a British Red Cross society in the United Kingdom. Furley had already been in touch with the International Committee of the Red Cross in Geneva over the desirability of founding a British national Red Cross society, and he knew that Lindsay also supported the goals of the new Red Cross movement. A letter from Loyd-Lindsay was published in *The Times* on 22 July calling for a national society in the United Kingdom, and pledging £1,000 of his own money to the new initiative.

British Ambulance Corps

The British Ambulance Corps was raised to serve with the Prussian forces, but also cared for captured French wounded during the siege of Paris of September 1870 to January 1871. The unit's B Division was commanded by surgeon William Manley VC, a British Army veteran of the Crimean and New Zealand wars and was attached to the Prussian Army's 22nd Division. The B Division tended to the wounded of the battles of Orléans (3–4 December), Cravant (10 December), Chateauneuf (18 December) and Bretoncelle (21 December). Manley was awarded the Iron Cross Second Class for his actions during the war, on the recommendation of Crown Prince Fredrick of Prussia who commanded the III Army (to which the 22nd Division belonged). He is the only man to receive both the British Victoria Cross and the German Iron Cross.

British ambulance stores at Metz. (*Illustrated London News*)

Franco-Irish Ambulance Brigade

The Franco-Irish Ambulance Brigade was commissioned by the Irish Committee for the Relief of the Sick and Wounded of the French Army and Navy on 7 September 1870. It sent 31 surgeons with 250 drivers and helpers to France, but the majority of the men were released on arrival as surplus to requirements. Many of the released men joined the French Foreign Legion and it has been alleged that the ambulance was used as a means of bypassing the Foreign Enlistment Act which prevented British subjects from enlisting in foreign armies.

The ambulance treated the wounded from a battle at Pacy-sur-Eure before being split into detachments serving with the Army of the North and the Army of the Loire. The detachments treated the wounded of the Volunteers at Châteaudun, Patay and Buchy and the First Battle of Orléans, the Battle of Loigny–Poupry and the Battle of Le Mans.

Public Fundraising in Britain

The United Kingdom remained neutral during the war, but numerous organisations were formed to provide medical assistance to one side or both. More than £300,000 of donations was made by the British public to provide for medical services during the conflict. Much of the funding went to 'ambulances' – a term that at the time referred to an organisation providing large-scale medical facilities including transport, field hospitals and surgical facilities rather than the more limited use of the word today. Many of the ambulances were staffed by doctors on leave from the British Army, with medical students from other nations serving on an ad-hoc basis.

Ambulances of Other Nations

Other neutral nations formed their own ambulances to provide medical assistance during the war, including the Netherlands, Italy, Austria, and Belgium. The regular medical facilities of both sides, together with the volunteer groups were never enough to cope with the almost unprecedented numbers of casualties caused by the weapons developed by 1870–1871. Records show that artillery fire was now the main reason for death and injuries on the battlefield. Rifle fire was secondary and cold steel was rarely, if ever, used.

Friends War Victims Relief Committee

The Friends War Victims Relief Committee (FWVRC) was an arm of British Quakers. It was first established in 1870, following the outbreak of the war and revived twice more (in Bulgaria in 1876 and in the Balkans in 1912) before being formally reconstituted at the outbreak of the First World War. It was revived for a fifth and final time in 1940, before its name was changed to the Friends Relief Service in 1941.

In 1870, the FWVRC undertook relief work in towns and villages devastated by the war. This was the first time the Quaker star was used as the badge of the Quaker relief worker, and the policy of giving aid equally to both sides was formally adopted.

FWVRC commissioners worked through the local communities in Paris, the Loire Valley and around Metz, providing emergency famine relief. It not only brought in food and essentials from Britain to war-torn France, but also gave practical aid by helping to plough fields ready for the harvest and bringing in steam ploughs to do the work. It was decided that a recognisable symbol was needed to identify the commissioners, their transport and the goods they carried. The red and black star of the Quaker relief worker was in fact the symbol of the *London Daily News*, which was then also funding relief work. The Quakers applied to share the symbol and added to it the words Quaker Relief Fund for Distressed Peasantry (in three languages).

Through the agency of 41 commissioners (33 men and eight women), the FWVRC undertook relief work among the civilian population of towns and villages devastated by the war. The commissioners were chosen for their knowledge of the country and the ability to speak French or German or both. They set out to help French and Germans equally, their policy being one of not discriminating between the opposing

Quaker volunteer nurses.

sides. The first operation centred on the town of Metz with the distribution of emergency supplies, the second on Paris after the end of the siege and the last in the Loire Valley which consisted of bringing in seeds to plant for a harvest the following year. The FWVRC also realised that a shortage of milk would lead to problems with children's health and resolved the situation by importing cows and goats to provide the necessary sustenance.

Losses

The Germans lost 1,046 officers and 16,539 NCOs and men killed, and a further 671 officers and 10,050 men died of their wounds, making a total loss of 28,306 killed. Typhoid and other diseases accounted for 207 officers and 11,940 men. Just over 4,000 men were accounted as missing and treated as killed in action or died on the battlefield. Several surgeons and at least one chaplain were among the dead. More than 88,000 officers and men suffered wounds. At least 50 officers and over 3,000 men were taken prisoner by the French. The Germans even counted the loss of 14,500 horses killed wounded and missing. The Field Railway Service lost 34 men killed wounded and missing and a further 14 were killed and 17 injured in accidents.

The French losses were a magnitude greater, with a total of 41,000 killed in action and 36,000 dying of wounds. A further 137,871 officers and men were wounded during the conflict. Over 383,000 French soldiers went into prison camps in Germany plus Bourbaki's army of 90,000 men was interred in Switzerland and at least 6,300 officers and men crossed the frontier into Belgium after the battle of Sedan.

Burying French soldiers outside the village of Chevilly, during the siege of Paris. (*Illustrated London News*)

Sickness

Typhus, Dysentery and Smallpox

Epidemics resulting from the war were also a major problem in 1870–1871. The army commanders and general doctors had underestimated the defence against epidemics. In August 1870 the German armies from the Saarbrück area advanced through Lorraine. Typhus (a bacterial infection spread by lice) and dysentery (also caused by bacteria in contaminated water) had long been endemic to these areas, as was known to the medical departments of the war ministries, but they had not taken any precautions. In a short period of time, epidemics affected the entire army. Providing soldiers hygiene was as yet a new idea for the regimental officers. Some 73,396 members of the German Army fell ill with typhus in 1870 and 38,652 with dysentery. The dysentery epidemic peaked in September and the typhus epidemic in October 1870. Fortunately, the incidences reduced by November. However, some field hospitals had to be converted into disease hospitals or new ones set up.

Before the outbreak of the war smallpox had broken out in parts of France but had remained localised. With the mobilisation of recruits for the French Army, the disease spread rapidly to other parts of the country, with devastating effects. By the end of 1870 no part of France had escaped its ravages. In 1868 there were over 4,100 deaths due to smallpox. So serious had the situation become, that in May 1870, two months before the outbreak of the war, a conference was called in Paris to plan the best means of controlling it. The best and really the only way to fight the disease was vaccination. Where vaccination had not been rigorously pursued, as in young children, the death rate was particularly high: in Paris out of a total 10,331 deaths during the years 1870–1871, 1,158 were less than a year old.

Records show that in the ten years to 1872, smallpox was responsible for a fifth of all deaths in the French Army. It is estimated that of the 600,000 French soldiers mobilised in the years 1870–1871 the number of smallpox cases was 125,000, of whom 23,470 died. The disease spread to the Prussian Army but had a limited effect as all Prussian recruits had been compulsorily inoculated since 1834. French prisoners incarcerated in camps in Prussia brought smallpox to the civilian population; French refugees took it to Belgium, and it quickly spread to the Netherlands. Garibaldi's troops returning to Italy after the war infected populations in Naples, Turin, Milan, and Genoa where 15,000 suffered and 3,500 died. It soon spread across Europe and Scandinavia, Austria and Russia and was even carried to the United States. French civilians fleeing to England carried the disease with them. In all it is estimated that over half a million died before the severity decreased and compulsory vaccination in many European countries brought better protection.

Wounds in Battle

From details gathered by the medical authorities on both sides of the conflict, it was estimated that the cause of wounds could be summarised that in every 100 cases, 70 were made by fragments of shell, and 30 by bullets; and further, that with regard to position of such wounds, 60 per cent of them were in the back or between the shoulders, and 40 in front or in the limbs. According to Doctor Steinberg, the Medical Officer in Chief of the Navy in charge of the military hospitals in Berlin, there were, by September 1871, 18,503 patients, of whom 8,531 were cases of wounds still unhealed. Of the latter number, 7,900 had been wounded by shot, 72 by swords and 96 by bayonets; and it may be further observed that of all the wounded taken care of in Berlin, no more than 261 died in hospital. There were invalided out of service some 2,598 men, but it must be noted that only the more slightly injured were sent all the way to Berlin.

Military 'experts', especially the more conservative officers, still advocated the use of 'cold steel' on the battlefield, but the very small numbers of those injured thus (barely 170 out of 7,900 nursed in the Berlin hospitals) shows how ineffective it was. Sword and bayonet were of importance not in their physical danger, but in their effect on morale when it came to close combat. As can be seen by the statistics the vast majority of casualties were killed or wounded at long range. Indeed a Prussian officer noted that he had received three bullet wounds without ever seeing an adversary.

According to official statistics, of 3,453 Germans wounded during the fighting around Metz, 95.5 per cent were struck by Chassepot bullets, 2.7 per cent by projectiles from artillery and only 0.8 per cent by bladed weapons. As for the French wounded, it was calculated that 25 percent were wounded by artillery fire and 70 percent by rifle fire. No fewer than 25,000 Frenchmen were struck by German artillery, giving one effective shot in three, as fired from their batteries. In the German Army, of every 100 men put out of action, 90 percent were in the infantry, 5 percent in the cavalry and 3 percent in the artillery. The total number of cartridges fired by the German infantryman in the war was about 25,000,000, or about 30 per man during the six months it lasted. Taking the total number of Frenchmen killed and wounded at 100,000, this would give 250 cartridges fired to each man hit.

The records of the war contain numerous accounts of the terrible effects of the *Mitrailleuse*, and instances are related of whole battalions and troops of cavalry having been all but completely swept away by its fire. Formidable though it was sometimes proved itself to be firing from cover, its effect in the open was disappointing. At Sedan, many batteries of the 'bullet squirt', as it was called by the Germans, were posted on the heights commanding Floing, but the damage they caused was inconsiderable. The growling noise of this weapon resembled nothing so much as the running of an anchor cable through a ship's cathead, or the closing of heavy iron shutters. Under such circumstances, however, as those in which the battles around Paris were fought, the full destructive power was scarcely tested. A considerable amount of the fighting took place so near the various villages extended around the city, in woods and otherwise upon such ground that the Germans seldom afforded an opportunity of putting the *Mitrailleuse* to the test. It was extensively used in the great sorties from Paris, especially in those of November and December across the Marne. Although it seemed to annihilate all within its immediate range, when the small extent of ground it covered and the compactness of its shower of its missiles often 'riddling' the same individual was more fully appreciated, it ceased to be so dreaded. However, under circumstances favouring their employment they occasionally created havoc in action: under General Manteuffel, a single volley delivered against his troops in action near Dijon is said to have killed and wounded 16 men. Such cases were very much the exception.

The conclusion arrived at regarding the *Mitrailleuse* was that it was a weapon for use at close quarters rather than battles that are fought at greater distances because the bullets do not spread out. Although it is undoubtedly a weapon of great destructive power, the *Mitrailleuse* fell short in of the ideal formed of it. The conclusion being that though having the potential for great damage, its deployment by the French was faulty and its design where the bullets were tightly grouped limited its destructive power.

The bullets of the *Mitrailleuse* are 40 mm long and 14 mm broad, rounded at the point and truncated behind. Their weight is 1¾ ounces.

Chapter 5

The Rest of the World

In the days before mobile telephones, television and radio, the only way to know what was happening in the world was by word of mouth; failing that one had to read eyewitness accounts in the newspapers. Papers were produced several times a day, as the news was updated. *The Times*, for instance, had morning and late editions each day. Some publishers had titles that appeared first thing and others that were printed for evening distribution. There were also weekly papers and specialist journals, and yet others with illustrations, produced by wood block printing. Every city had several publications, usually with some political bias, and even small provincial towns had their own paper. This was particularly prevalent in the English-speaking world, where even a Midwestern American paper and a small town in New Zealand would carry 'News of the War' within its pages, alongside the latest market prices for pork and barley.

As soon as war was declared newspaper correspondents flooded into France and Germany trying to obtain fresh news of events for their readers. They were generally referred to as 'specials'. Their reports were often written up either during the conflict, or very soon after and many were later published in book form. Some correspondents were less successful in reporting the news and their reports are filled with accounts of difficult travels.[1] Some reports are less than useful in illuminating what was happening on the ground – either the newsmen were always just too late in observing a battle or were busy telling their readers about the poor state of the hotels, lack of proper food and obstructiveness of the authorities.

The problems of war reporting were exemplified by the German writer Theodor Fontane who, while having what he thought were suitable papers, was arrested by enthusiastic *gendarmes* and flung into prison in Besançon, accused of spying. Some reporters were amateurs when it came to understanding what was going on in front of their eyes, while others were experienced soldiers or ex-soldiers and gave a reliable account of the war. As well as newspaper reporters there were also official agents of various governments who were tasked with giving information to their ministers at home. If they were lucky, they could get an attachment to the staff of a senior officer and thus be in a position to have good view of events. Colonel Beauchamp Walker was the British military attaché in Berlin and formed a personal relationship with the Prussian crown prince and was part of his entourage during the Austrian war in 1866 and the campaign in France and during the siege of Paris.

Colonel Otto Corvin, a scion of a noble family, had been a junior officer in the Prussian Army before becoming a revolutionary in Paris in 1848 and in Baden in 1849 and later, after his release from prison, a reporter during the American Civil War. His knowledge of German, French and English and his understanding of military technicalities made his reports for the English, German and American press full of interest. He also had many acquaintances among the German military and ruling houses which gained

1 The French military authorities were very reticent to allow foreign civilians anywhere near the fighting, fearing they were all spies. The Germans were also less than keen to have civilians getting in the way of their operations but did authorise a few individuals to accompany some units in the field.

Anton von Werner, noted German war artist and painter, wearing his campaigning gear, 1870.
(Engraving from an original photograph)

Heinrich Lüders, noted German artist, drawing at night in his quarters, 1870.

him access to sources that lesser mortals could not obtain. He paid a visit to the Prussian crown prince at Versailles and observed his staff; as commander of the Third Army the prince had his chief of staff, Lieutenant-General von Blumenthal, and a chief quartermaster together with their staffs, but as a royal prince he also had a court under a court-marshal and a first aide-de-camp. The Third Army included contingents from the south German states, who were represented on the crown prince's staff.

Others following the crown prince included Colonel Beauchamp Walker and a multitude of princes: the Duke of Coburg, the Crown Prince of Wurttemberg, the princes of Saxe-Weimar and Mecklenburg, and the unfortunate Prince Leopold of Hohenzollern, who had been the innocent cause of the war. What is now called the 'Press Pack' followed this glittering array, including William Russell (of Crimean War fame) of *The Times* and John Edwin Hilary Skinner of the *Daily News*, together with several German correspondents, the German artist Georg Bleibtreu and the English artist Robert Landells whose work was reproduced in the *Illustrated London News.*

William Russell of *The Times* was already a famous man. His reputation for fearless reporting had been established during the Crimean War where he had seen and reported on the shocking state of the British Army and the conditions under which it fought. His first war reports were sent from Denmark when he accompanied the Schleswig-Holstein forces in 1850. He had observed the Battle of Koniggratz in 1866 and made contacts with several German officers. *The Times* sent him to Europe in 1870, although he was

William Howard Russell of *The Times,* 1870. (*The Graphic*)

constantly 'scooped' by Forbes. He continued to use the *Feldpost* and the mail to get his dispatches back to London, even though his editor pressed him to make more use of the telegraph.

While Russell was perhaps, 'the first and greatest of war correspondents', Archibald Forbes of the *Daily News* was the luckiest. He seemed to sense where the news was and during the early part of the war argued that wherever Bismarck was there was his story. After the Battle of Sedan he saw the Prussian chancellor riding across the countryside and decided to follow him. Soon there appeared an open carriage on the road containing four French officers. Forbes recognised one of them as Napoleon himself and watched as Napoleon and Bismarck stopped at a cottage awaiting the arrival of the king of Prussia to accept the French surrender. He shared the scoop with his travelling companion, a young Dutchman, Jacob de Liefde who was sending his reports to the *Glasgow Herald*.

Archibald Forbes had been at university at Aberdeen before moving to Edinburgh and then on to London where he heard lectures given by William Russell. This determined him on a military career, and he enlisted in the Royal Dragoons. However, military life was not all charging about a battlefield, and he became the schoolteacher to his company and acting quartermaster-sergeant, while sending short pieces on military life to the newspapers. Unfortunately, his health broke down and he spent some months in a military hospital. The newspapers were his real interest, and he started a paper of his own, the *London Scotsman*, of which he was owner, editor, and sole contributor. He also created a weekly paper entitled *Anglo-Scottish News*, which ran from July 1867 until January 1871. He published a novel based on the Indian Mutiny, mostly drawn from the memory of a veteran of the campaign. The battle scenes in the novel so impressed James Grant (another Scotsman) of the *Morning Advertiser* that he commissioned Forbes to go to the seat of the war and he immediately set off first buying suitable campaigning clothes and with £20 in cash in his pocket for expenses. By various means he got his stories back to London by using the German *Feldpost*, sending his dispatches back to the nearest town in Prussia and leaving a sum of money with the telegraph manager at Saarbruck to transmit to London. After the French surrender and the subsequent rising of the Commune in Paris, he managed to gain access to the city to write about conditions and was nearly executed by the Communards as a spy, being 'fortunately' rescued by the French Versailles Army who took him for a Communard and he was nearly shot for a second time until rescued by an officer.

Apart from the problems of accommodation and finding food, battlefields can be dangerous places. One of *The Times* correspondents who was with the crown prince of Saxony at the Battle of Sedan asked the prince if he could observe from a part of the battlefield that appeared to be unoccupied. Lieutenant-Colonel Christopher Pemberton, recently retired as a regular officer in the Scots Fusilier Guards, with an escort of Saxon staff guards rode a quarter of a mile or so from the crown prince's position and was suddenly confronted by several French infantrymen, one of whom fired and shot Pemberton through the head. There followed a small skirmish between the Saxon cavalry and some French horsemen. The body of the colonel was later found, his effects already plundered, and was buried by the side of the road.

Another British officer present at the Battle of Sedan was Major Sir Henry Havelock VC, who was the son of the general of the same name who had gained fame in India. Havelock was awarded his Victoria Cross during the Indian Mutiny as a young lieutenant leading his battalion in action. He went to France, after taking leave of absence from the army, and acted as an 'occasional correspondent' for several papers.

Some specials limited themselves to a specific army or campaign, while reporting to several papers. Edward Henry Vizetelly, had been educated in France and not only signed up to report upon the war for the *Daily News* and the *New York Times*, but also joined Garibaldi's Army of the Vosges as a staff officer. The Vizetelly family introduced five members into the newspaper world, the father being one of the founders of the *Illustrated London News*. The youngest son, Ernest Alfred Vizetelly was only 17 when he went with his father to France. He sent reports back to London to the *Daily News*, the *Pall Mall Gazette* and as an artist he also reported to the *Illustrated London News*. When his father returned to England he carried on as a correspondent on his own account, following Chanzy's Second Army of the Loire to Le Mans and sending a long account to his brother in London who passed it on to the newspapers for publication.

Archibald Forbes of the *Daily News,* 1870. (*The Graphic*)

Mr G.T. Robinson of the *Manchester Guardian,* 1870. (*The Graphic*)

Sir Randal Howland Roberts was born in 1837 in Britfieldstown, Co. Cork, the son of Sir Thomas Howland Roberts, 3rd Baronet of Glassenbury and Britfieldstown. When his father died in 1864, Roberts succeeded him as the 4th Baronet. Roberts attended the Merchant Taylors' School before entering the army. He served in the Crimea and in the Indian Mutiny before retiring. He then turned to journalism, writing on military and sporting topics, and acting as a war correspondent for the *Daily Telegraph* during the Franco–Prussian War. For the opening battles of the war, he associated himself with the Prussian 33rd Regiment and shared their rations and marches (but on horseback, of course). He acquired a position on the staff of the Prussian General von Goeben of the First Army and accompanied it throughout the war. His book of the campaign, *Modern War*, includes the following:

> [On Prussian soldiers at Saarbruck]: 'These men, who marched without stockings, many in new boots of untanned leather, would have done some of our generals' hearts good to see. Their feet are wrapped in a greasy cloth, two pairs of which, with a bottle of grease, comprise a portion of each man's kit in his knapsack.'
>
> [Criticism of the French press]: 'The fulsome report that the Emperor sent to the Empress, which was published in a French newspaper, stating that the town of Saarbruck had been taken, although defended by a body of 20,000 Prussians – the troops in Saarbruck being actually only 952 strong – now reached the head-quarters of the 1st Army, and afforded immense amusement to every one. This was the commencement of those tissues of falsities that misled the people of France and emanated from the French press.'
>
> [Bivouacking in the field]: 'When the regiment is halted the arms are piled, the battalions being drawn up in line of contiguous columns at battalion distance; the men then take off their helmets, and each man places it on his rifle, which acts as an effectual protection from any wet getting down the barrel; they put on their forage-caps, and the companies then break off by subdivisions to the right and left of their arms, the knapsacks are placed in a row, the camp kettles taken off, and the fatigue squad meantime … dig small oblong holes in the ground for their fires; a couple of sticks at each end, and another resting across, completes the simple but practical arrangement. On this stick hang the camp kettles, generally speaking by twos – one for the potatoes, and the other for the soup and meat.
>
> One of the most imposing features in this bivouac in the woods was the "Zapfen Streich", or the Last Post, played by the band of each regiment. First of all, a roll on the drum called your attention, then the Post was magnificently played, and lastly the evening hymn.'
>
> [Description of a Prussian sutler's wife]: 'A French soldier's cap covered her grizzled hair, the peak shading a face which, from exposure to the sun, looked like a piece of badly-tanned leather; a voltigeur's jacket enveloped her body, and a large red bandanna was wound round her waist, where she carried a huge knife, with which to cut the hard black bread into the pieces she dispensed to the soldiers; her arms and hands were brown-black, partly from exposure and partly from dirt; whilst, to complete her semi-military costume, the shortness of her petticoat revealed her feet encased in a pair of long boots that had once been the property of some Prussian soldier. If you were in favour, madame produced a piece of meat from the recesses of the wagon, and perhaps an onion, a piece of bread, and a glass of schnapps, for which you paid the moderate sum of one thaler.'
>
> [There were compensations, for even in the field]: 'The band was really the luxury of the day. It played in the afternoon, and the delicious airs of Beethoven, Mozart and Meyerbeer transported you in imagination far from the surrounding scenes (of death and destruction).'

How did the stories of the battles come to appear in newspapers in England and almost as quickly in America? George W. Smalley, who had reported on the American Civil War for the *New York Tribune*, relates the instructions he had received from his editor. The system used initially was for 'the special' to write his account and post it to London, not trusting to the telegraph which could be read by anyone and was often subject to censorship. However, it soon became clear that sending a cable was the swiftest way of communicating. Smalley's method was to use the telegraph to send an account of any preliminary fights, but to make their way back to London writing a detailed account on arrival. One of his agents, Moncure D. Conway, observed the Battle of Gravelotte from the position occupied by King Wilhelm and his staff and afterwards walked the battlefield with another American reporter and Archibald Forbes. Following instructions Conway set off to London to file his story. First by peasant cart to a town 12 miles away, then by wagon to Saarbruck to find a train. He was not allowed on the train as it was carrying wounded back to Germany. Undaunted he climbed onto the top of one of the cars as the train left the station. He spent ten hours thus transported, took another train to Treves and stagecoach to Luxembourg, then on to Brussels, arriving at Ostend in time for the night ferry and was in London by morning. The story of Gravelotte was cabled to America for the pages of the *New York World* and a second version appeared in the *Daily News*, which was distributed all over Europe and translated into every language.

American citizens departing from Paris, autumn 1870. (*The Graphic*)

War artists sketching in the field.

The Battle of Sedan, which proved the pivotable point of the war, was fought on Thursday, 1 September and a special, one of Smalley's agents, Mr Holt White, arrived at the newspaper office in London the following Saturday afternoon. He there and then wrote the account for the *New York Tribune* and another for the *Pall Mall Gazette*. The New York paper published the story on Sunday morning, but the English paper only had an afternoon edition so was second with the news. On Monday afternoon, the special, M. Mejanel walked into Smalley's office with an account of Sedan as seen from the French side. He had been with Napoleon's army, was captured by the Prussians, and somehow escaped and made his way to the Channel and then to London. Mejanel was also a talented artist, and his sketches of the Battle of Sedan were worked up into an illustration for the *Graphic*.

As well as the cost of sending telegrams (they had to be paid for by the word), in 1866 Smalley sent a cable from Berlin of about 100 words which cost him $500 at the time, an enormous amount. Specials were well rewarded for their efforts. The newspapers handed over great sums of money to pay the telegraph operators, buy food and accommodation, and bribe officials, if necessary. However, the rewards for the papers were considerable. After publishing the report of the Battle of Sedan, the daily circulation of the *Daily News* jumped from 50,000 copies to 150,000, a threefold increase. The *New York Herald*, dated Monday 18 July, carried a series of dispatches dated to the afternoon of the 17th. One dispatch reports a rumour that a great battle had been fought near Forbach and that the French government had denied recalling its troops from Rome. A clarification published in the *Worcester Evening Gazette*, Worcester, Massachusetts, on 22 July states that the 'great battle' was no more than an exchange of shots at the Forbach customs posts.

The French paper, *Le Gaulois*, carried the reports from Sedan on Sunday, 4 September, together with comments from the Belgian papers, *L'Independence belge* and the *Peuple belge*, the latter of which reported:

> A persistent rumour, and which we can however give only with all reservations, has been circulating since this morning; it is affirmed that a Prussian corps, which would have crossed the Belgian frontier, and if summoned to surrender, would have replied with gunshots. An engagement would have followed in which 600 of ours would have perished, while 1,500 Prussians would have been taken prisoner. This would explain the departure of the Brussels garrison for the border.

Le Gaulois, on the following day carried the news of the capture of Napoleon, MacMahon and 40,000 men. However, it says that the report comes from Belgium from the correspondent of the *Pall Mall Gazette*.

Foreign Observers

Colonel Beauchamp Walker

Walker was commissioned as ensign in the 33rd foot on 27 February 1836, becoming lieutenant on 21 June 1839 and captain on 22 December 1846. He served with that regiment at Gibraltar, the West Indies, and North America. On 16 November 1849 he transferred into the 7th Dragoon Guards. On 25 March 1854 he was appointed aide-de-camp to Lord Lucan, who commanded the cavalry division in the army sent to the Crimea. He was present at Alma, Balaclava, and Inkerman, and was mentioned in despatches. In the middle of October, he acted as aide-de-camp to Lord George Paulet on board the *Bellerophon*. This qualified him for the medal for naval service, as well as the Crimean medal with four clasps, the Turkish medal and the Medjidie (fifth class). On 7 December 1858 he became lieutenant-colonel of the 2nd Dragoon Guards. He joined that regiment in India and took part in the later operations for the suppression of the Mutiny. From India he went on to China, being appointed on 14 May 1860 assistant quartermaster-general of cavalry in Sir Hope Grant's expedition. On 26 April 1865 he was made military attaché to the embassy at Berlin, a post he held for nearly 12 years. In the Austro–Prussian War of 1866 he was attached to the headquarters of the crown prince's army as British military commissioner; he witnessed the Battles of Nachod and Königgratz. Walker was again attached to the crown prince's army in the Franco–German War and was present at Weissenburg, Wörth, Sedan, and throughout the siege of Paris. He was given the campaign medal and the Iron Cross. Unlike the newspaper reporters, his task was to represent the British Government and keep the War Office in England informed as to the campaign's progress and convey official British policy to the Prussian crown prince. Walker's verdict on the Prussian cavalry and their new division structure was extremely positive, although it cannot be ruled out that Walker wanted to emphasise the importance of his own branch of service.

Colonel Beauchamp Walker, British military attaché in Berlin and joined the staff of the Prussian Crown in France.

General Philip Sheridan

In late July 1870, President Grant agreed to Major General Philip Sheridan's request to be an observer during the war. Sheridan and one of his aides, James W. Forsyth (an old companion dating back to the Virginia Campaigns of 1864–1865) sailed to Europe and caught up with the Prussian forces in August. He travelled as a guest of Chancellor Otto von Bismarck and King Wilhelm of Prussia. In this capacity he witnessed some of the largest battles of the war and was present for Napoleon's surrender. During the early operations around Paris, he met the US ambassador to France, Elihu Washburne, Brigadier General William Hazen and Major General Ambrose Burnside. Twice his blue US uniform frock coat was mistaken for French, and he was nearly killed by German soldiers. He observed and wrote about what was perceived as a change in the doctrine of how Prussian soldiers fought: '[T]he scattered condition while engaged, the men engaged on both sides were so scattered that it looked like thousands of men engaged in a deadly skirmish without any regard to lines, or formations. These battles were of this style of fighting, commencing at long range and might be called "progressive fighting".'[2] Sheridan was observing the effects of Prussian infantry tactics on the battlefield as small-sized units, even half-companies, executed offensive movements against larger massed French forces. The superior use of weapons (especially artillery) and the decentralised tactics of the Prussians overwhelmed the concentrated French lines and displayed what Sheridan could only comprehend as chaos. The 'progressive fighting' Sheridan described dubiously in his correspondence to Grant foreshadowed how units would fight in the next great continental fight: small-unit manoeuvre combining fire and movement to overwhelm and destroy the enemy forces versus the Napoleonic era doctrine of concentrated mass against the decisive point. Sheridan's travels also took him to Vienna, Constantinople, Italy and back to France in time for the war's formal end, after which he returned to the United States visiting England on the way.

General Ambrose Burnside

Colonel Frank Moore, the Second Secretary of the United States Legation, had taken the last diplomatic pouch out of Paris before the siege began and delivered it at the US Embassy in London. General Burnside (he of the impressive side whiskers) and Colonel Paul Forbes came to Europe, it seems of their own volition,

2 Philip H. Sheridan, *The Personal Memoirs of P. H. Sheridan*, volume 2, (New York: Charles L. Webster & Co, 1888).

to act as observers and set out from London for Paris in late September, taking with them a diplomatic pouch. They persuaded the Germans that they could be useful as neutral intermediaries and asked permission to cross the lines and enter Paris. Not only did they get passes from the Germans, but they also talked their way into Paris using the delivery of the diplomatic pouch as an excuse. They had an interview with the commander of the Paris army, General Trochu, and returned to German headquarters with the French proposals for an armistice. However, the negotiations came to nothing as each side would make no concessions at this stage.

The Swiss Federal Army Defends Its Neutrality

Switzerland had a unique system of government: it was made up of 26 individual states, termed 'cantons' who had, before 1848, been independent of each other. Political tensions in the 1840s, between conservative Catholics and liberal Protestants, led in 1847 to the outbreak of war between two groups of cantons. The more numerous liberal cantons were victorious and in 1848 a new constitution was drawn up which bound all the cantons together within a more structured union. One of the conditions was the prohibition of the new federation from having a standing army. However, all adult citizens were obliged to serve in the federal army if called to do so. If required, a force of 80,000 men could be mobilised. There was, however, a small cadre of officers who were the only men to serve full time. In the war between the cantons, the Sonderbund War, the representatives of each side selected an officer to be their commander in chief, for the federal side it was Henri Dufour, an engineer officer from Geneva. In 1870 the army was mobilised and Hans Herzog, an artilleryman, was elected general. He had served during the Sonderbund War and then gone into the family business. In 1860 he rejoined the army and was appointed Inspector-General of Artillery. As the commander of the Swiss army on the border in the Jura Mountains he concluded a convention with the French General Clinchant for the internment of the French Army of the East. The Swiss disarmed the French troops, but as part of the agreement had to return the weapons to the French government in 1871.

Each canton supplied a contingent of troops according to its population, based on the structure of the battalion and half-battalion in the infantry and on the company in the dragoons. The artillery was composed of separate batteries and the engineers by company. The largest canton, Berne, supplied 24 infantry battalions; nine 'sharpshooter' or *jäger* companies; nine companies of dragoons and nine batteries of artillery; four companies of sappers and two of pontooniers. Uri, one of the smallest cantons, contributed a half-battalion of infantry, plus two detached companies and two companies of sharpshooters.

The permanent staff of the army was composed of 76 colonels, 93 lieutenant-colonels, 130 majors, 226 captains and 292 lieutenants. The Swiss male population was enrolled at the age of 20 in the '*Auszug*', or 'Active Levy', where they received five weeks training before being sent home, to be recalled biannually for a 12-day refresher. At the age of 34 they transferred to the Reserve for a period of six years and then into the *Landwehr* for a further five years. In an emergency all male citizens, not in the Active Levy, the Reserve or the *Landwehr* are called out as the '*Landsturm*'.

The Active Levy and Reserve formed 106 battalions of infantry, 19 half-battalions, 22 detached companies and 74 *jäger* companies. The cavalry had seven companies of mounted guides, 35 of dragoons, the artillery 50 field batteries and 12 companies of sappers. In theory this would provide an army of 120,000 men, to which a force of 50,000 *Landwehr* men could be added.

The battalions were organised into brigades, three of which formed a division of which nine could be called out for service. In 1851 the Swiss infantry were armed with a muzzle-loading rifle which was altered to breech-loading in 1867, using the '*tabatière*' system similar to the French rifles. However, the authorities were already looking at a breech-loading bolt-action rifle and had settled on the Vetterli Model 1867. Its advanced design incorporated a 12-round magazine in a tube under the barrel similar to the American Winchester rifle. Johann Friedrich Vetterli trained as a gunsmith and had later worked in France and England, while in London he met and married Charlotte Fryman. He became acquainted with the armament producer Friedrich Peyer im Hof and designed a bayonet rolling mill for him. In 1867 he invented a new rifle and the metallic case ammunition to go with it. Vetterli improved the bolt even as the rifle was put into production which became the Model 1868. He then changed the position of the cleaning rod which went into mass production as the Model 1869. His rifles were continuously improved both in Switzerland and Italy, and some Italian models were even (re-)issued during the First World War.

The Swiss infantry uniform looked very similar to the French one with a double-breasted blue tunic although without any coloured distinctions. The full trousers were also blue, and the double-breasted great-coat had red tabs on the collar. The leather shako had a front and back peak and a leather chinstrap. The jager had a similar uniform, but in place of the shako, wore a black round hat decorated with cock's feathers. Equipment was of black leather. All Swiss troops of whatever branch wore, on the upper left sleeve, an armband of red cloth with a small white cross when on active service. Swiss battalions each carried the national emblem, a red sheet with a white cross with the arms extending to the edge of the material. On the white horizontal bar, the name of the canton appeared in gold letters.

Artists Depicting the War

The war between France and Prussia in 1870–1871 attracted considerable attention from the world's press and numerous journalists flocked to France to cover the fighting and the subsequent events in and around Paris culminating in the Commune. The *Illustrated London News* dispatched two artists, William Simpson (1823–1899) and Robert Thomas Landells (1833–1877), and their numerous sketches were sent back to London and engraved as woodcuts for printing in the weekly issues of the newspaper. Some of Landells' sketches were flown out of the besieged city by balloon post.

William Simpson is widely known known today as the war artist whose first-hand depiction of the Crimean War helped bring home the reality of that ill-managed campaign to the British public. As a 'camp follower' (for such was, strictly, a description of war artists) Simpson later accompanied the British Army to Abyssinia with General Napier in 1868 to free the hostages being held by Emperor Theodorus. Simpson covered the war in 1870 and managed to follow closely the Germans as they advanced and entered Strasbourg and Metz (in the process being arrested as a spy). He covered the Paris Commune the following year.

The technique used at the time was for the artist to produce a fairly rough draft of the event being reported upon, with notes added to explain or enlarge details. The sketch was sent to London by the postal service or whatever means were the quickest and then for a skilled artist, the *Illustrated London News*'s Arthur Hopkins for example, to lay out the sketch on a block (or blocks) of wood and use a sharp point to mark the outlines, in reverse. The artist then had to carve the picture in the wood, in effect, the wrong way round, so when the block was fitted in the frame for printing it would appear the right way.[3]

Robert Landells was the son of Ebenezer Landells who had started *Punch* magazine and was an engraver for the *Illustrated London News* when it was first published. In 1856 Landells was sent by the *Illustrated London News* as special artist to the Crimea and contributed some illustrations of the close of the campaign. After the peace he went to Moscow for the coronation of Tzar Alexander II and contributed illustrations of the ceremony. He was present as artist throughout the war between Germany and Denmark in 1864, receiving decorations from both sides, and again in the war between Austria and Prussia in 1866. On the latter occasion he was attached to the staff of the crown prince of Prussia. On the outbreak of the Franco–German war in 1870 he was again attached to the staff of the crown prince, and during the siege of Paris resided at the prince's headquarters in Versailles. He received an award not only for his labours as

3 One does occasionally see names or lettering that appears to be backwards in the final print, a slip by the artist or his assistant!

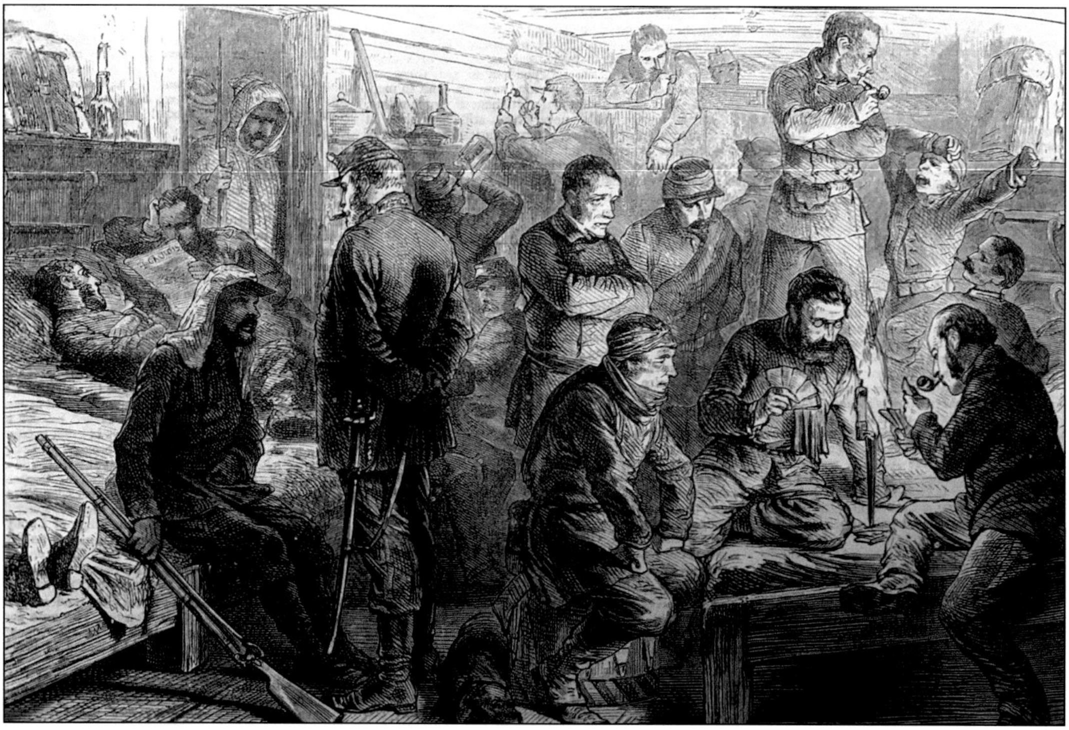

French Gardes Nationale off-duty. (*The Graphic*)

an artist, but for his assistance to the ambulances as well as the Bavarian cross for valour. Landells was also a respected painter.

Popular Culture

Fashion

The style of ladies' fashions was not immune from the influence of the war, although the 'Latest Fashions from Paris' which were a regular feature of English language journals was interrupted, albeit with at least one illustration showing a ladies riding habit with decoration to the bodice *à la hussar*, with black braid to the front and back.

Music

The British music halls and drawing rooms of private houses were deluged with up-to-date tunes and ditties and piano pieces all reflecting the news from France. For the price of three or four shillings (15 or 20 pence) new tunes such as 'The Prince Frederick William March', a piece of sheet music illustrated with a lifelike portrait of the prince, or 'Just Before the Battle' a descriptive fantasia by Alfred Mullen at 1/6d (7 pence) could be obtained. Mullen also penned 'The King William March', introducing the song 'I am a Prussian' as sung by the Royal Prussian Guards. 'L'Echo de la Guerre' was even handed as it was based on the 'Prussian March' and the 'Marseillaise' was based on a work by 'Chevalier de Kontski' as performed on his provincial tour. Metzler and Company published a clutch of tunes with the covers illustrated with pictures of the German lancers: 'The Uhlan Quadrille' and 'The Uhlan Galop' and the fearsomely entitled 'The Armourers of the Rhine'.

Women's fashions for 1870.

Cover from a sheet music score, 'Uhlan's Quadrille'.

Bibliography and Further Reading

This list includes some of the works referred to in the preparation of this book, along with critical comments.

Amicale de Collectionneurs de Figurines Historiques, 'Les Zouaves Pontificaux dans la guerre de 1870–1871', special issue (number 32) of *Le Briquet*, December 2020. Lots of information packed into this paperback booklet, including colour illustrations and photographs of uniforms. In French.

Belleval, René de, *Journal d'un capitaine de francs-tireurs* (Paris: Lachaud, 1872). In French.

Bordone, Philippe Toussaint Joseph, *Garibaldi et L'Armee des Vosges* (Paris, 1871). Official report of Garibaldi's army on campaign written by his Chief of Staff. In French.

Boyland, George Halstead, *Six Months under the Red Cross, with the French Army* (Cincinnati, OH: Robert Clarke & Co., 1873). An American volunteer doctor serving with the Army of the Rhine and shut up in Metz during the siege and later with the Army of the Loire.

Bulletin Officiel Du Ministere de L'Interieur, issue number 9 for August 1870. Official announcements, correspondence, orders and decrees issued by the French government. Particularly useful for instructions for raising, maintaining, arming and equipping the *Gardes Mobiles*. Available on the '*gallica*' website of the French National Library. Other issues of the *Bulletin* deal with further details of volunteer units. In French.

Corvin, Otto (in full: Otto Julius Bernhard von Corvin-Wiersbitzki), *In France with the Germans*, 2 volumes (London, 1872). The author was a colourful character, a former Prussian officer, an author (he wrote a popular book on swimming), a revolutionary, fighting in Paris in 1848 and Baden in 1849, where he received the rank of colonel. Sentenced to death, commuted to six years solitary confinement. He reported on the American Civil War for *The Times* and later on the Franco–German War for British, American and German newspapers.

Doehler, R., *Prussia's Medical Service in the Wars of Unification*, in *Wehrmedizin und Wehrpharmazie* (Bonn, 2016). Background to the Prussian medical services by the modern research centre of the German Army. In English.

Edwards, H. Sutherland, *The Germans in France: Notes on the Method and Conduct of the Invasion, the Relations between Invaders and Invaded, and the Modern Usages of War* (London, 1874). Written by one of *The Times* reporters at the scene of the war and who took the trouble to check up on supposed reports of brutality; also includes a discussion on the 'rules of war'.

Engels, Frederick, 'The Rationale of the Prussian Army System', *Pall Mall Gazette*, 8 October 1870.

Engels Frederick, 'Notes on the War', *Pall Mall Gazette*, 29 July 1870–18 February 1871. Transcribed in the Marxists Internet Archive. Engels had some limited experience of campaigning, having served as a volunteer during the 1848 uprising in Baden. His reports showed that he had considerable insight in the military conditions of the war, although tempered with his political philosophy.

Franco-German War 1870–71, The Second Part: History of the War against the Republic. German official account, translated by Major F.C. Clarke in 1884 and reprinted in 1996 by the Battery Press, Nashville, TN. Enormous amount of detail, especially, of course, from the German side, with footnotes, appendices, orders of battle and a few maps. In five volumes, Volume 5 is particularly rich in statistics and totals for the war.

Gestin, Robert, *Memories of the Army of Brittany* (1908). The chief medical officer of the Army of Brittany, so a first-hand account sympathetic to the Bretons and their commander, General Kératry.

Gordon, Charles Alexander, *Lessons on Hygiene and Surgery from the Franco-Prussian War* (London, 1873). Includes chapters on hygiene, war hospitals, wounds caused by different arms, feeding and clothing of soldiers and hospital diets. Doctor Gordon, the Deputy Inspector-General of Hospitals, was sent by the British government to observe and report on French medical services. He also had access to many official publications from both sides.

Hazen, W.B. Brevet Major-General, *The School and the Army in Germany and France: With a Diary of Siege Life at Versailles* (New York: Harper & Brothers/London: Trubner & Co., 1873). American official observer with access to Bismarck, the crown prince and state ministries in Berlin. Contains personal anecdotes of life during the siege of Paris, from the German lines, of course.

Home, Robert, *A Precis of Modern Tactics* (London, 1882). It describes itself as: 'A Précis of Modern Tactics: Compiled from the Works of Recent Continental Writers at the Topographical and Statistical Department of the War Office'. Covers the period from Frederick the Great to the Franco–German War, with text and diagrams.

Howland Roberts, Randal, *Modern War: The Campaigns of the First Prussian Army, 1870–71* (London, 1871). Howland Roberts served as a war correspondent for the *Daily Telegraph* and, for his various services in this period, he was awarded the Iron Cross of Prussia, made a Knight of the Legion of Honour and a Knight of St Maurice and Lazarus of Italy.

La Guerre de 1870–71, La Defense Nationale en Province, Vol. Mesures Generals d'Organisation (Paris: Historical Section of the General Staff of the French Army, 1911). Review of the restructuring of the French Army and the raising of the new armies after the battle of Sedan. In French.

Lecomte, Ferdinand, *Relation historique et critique de la Guerre Franco-Allemande en 1870–1871, Vol. 4* (Paris, 1874). The author was a colonel in the Swiss Federal Army. An account of the war, but with appendices covering orders of battle, text of the convention with the Swiss to inter the French Army of the East and other documents. Four maps attached to the inside back cover. In French.

Mauni, Roger de, *The Franco-Prussian War* (London: Longman, 1970). Originally published as *Eight Months on Duty: The Diary of a Young Officer in Chanzy's Army* (London, 1872). Roger de Mauni volunteered to serve as a private soldier in the ranks of the Paris *Garde Mobile* of the Seine, transferring to the *Garde Mobile* of Normandy, designated as the Battalion of Mortain, part of the 30th *Régiment de Marche*, with the rank of lieutenant. A soldier's eye view of the campaign on the Loire: constant marching without any apparent plan, cold, wet and hungry.

Martinien, A., *La Guerre de 1870–1871: La mobilisation de l'Armee* (Paris, 1911). Several volumes. The author worked for the French Army Historical Section of the General Staff. He produced many statistical works from official records covering the First Empire and the war of 1870–1871. In French.

Pratt, Edwin A., *The Rise of Rail-Power in War and Conquest, 1833–1914* (Philadelphia, PA and London, 1916). The author was a British journalist (ten years with *The Times*); a prolific writer of biographies and works on railways, canals, agriculture, alcohol licensing, trades unions, and so on. His book has chapters on German and French railways and how they were used during the war. Good analysis of the subject.

Roberts, Randal H., *Modern War, or the Campaigns of the First Prussian Army, 1870–71* (London: Chapman & Hall, 1871).

Ruckert, Carl, *Carl Ruckert's Memoirs of the Franco-Prussian War*, Translated, edited and with an introduction by Alfred Kelly (Cham, 2019). A view from the German side. Ruckert was a one-year volunteer in the Hessian Army with the rank of lance corporal. Like Roger de Mauni, he reported constant marching with little idea of what the plan was. He was badly wounded at the battle of Gravelotte and suffered amputation of the leg. An interesting first-hand account of the German medical services.

Showalter, Dennis E., *The Wars of German Unification* (London: Bloomsbury, 2004). The writer was for many years Professor of History at Colorado College and the author of numerous books on all aspects of military history. The chapters on 'The War against the Empire' and 'The Republic Strikes Back' are full of information and insights on both the French and German ways of dealing with the new circumstances they encountered. Written in a very open and interesting style, a pleasure to read.

Showalter, Dennis E., 'Prussian Cavalry, 1806–1871: The Search for Roles', *Militärgeschichtliche Zeitschrift*, 19:1 (2014).

United States Army, 'Translation of the German General Staff "History of the German-French War 1870–71"', *Journal of the Military Service Institution of the United States* (New York, 1882). The translation of the German account covering the period from the beginning of September until the end of the war. Not an account of the war, but lots of facts and figures on the support services, ammunition supplies and so on.

Walker, Charles Pyndar Beauchamp, *Days of a Soldier's Life* (London, 1894). In 1865, Walker was appointed British military attaché to the embassy at Berlin, a post he held until 1876. During the Austro–Prussian War of 1866 and the Franco–German War of 1870–1871 he acted as British military commissioner to the crown prince of Prussia's army and was present at the battles of Weissenburg, Wörth and Sedan as well as the siege of Paris. He became a personal friend of the Prussian crown prince, who later became the second emperor of Germany.

Walter, Dierk, *A Military Revolution? Prussian Military Reforms before the Wars of German Unification* (Oslo: Institutt for Forsvarsstudier, 2001). A modern analysis.

West, Leonard and Guy, A.-R., *The Dreyse Military Needle-Ignition System: An Illustrated History* (Bognor Regis: Woodfield, 2019). Monograph on all things Dreyse, lavishly illustrated by the authors.

Many of the contemporary works cited are long out of print and paper copies can be difficult to obtain. However, a large number of nineteenth-century books are available as digital copies on various internet sites. As ever, the French National Library under its '*gallica*' website is an absolute mine of information; its one million plus collection of books, pamphlets and pictures are all available in digital form and freely downloadable. The collection includes German and English works as well as French originals.

The Wikipedia site on the internet is self-policed in terms of accuracy of information, so always treat its articles with care. But it contains articles on almost any subject you can think of, and many that you have not!